AMBASSADOR FOR
LIBERTY

To order additional copies of *Ambassador for Liberty,*
by Bert B. Beach,
call **1-800-765-6955**.

Visit us at
www.reviewandherald.com
for information on other Review and Herald® products.

AMBASSADOR FOR LIBERTY

Building Bridges of Faith, Friendship, and Freedom

BERT B. BEACH

REVIEW AND HERALD® PUBLISHING ASSOCIATION
Since 1861 | www.reviewandherald.com

Copyright © 2012 by Review and Herald® Publishing Association

Published by Review and Herald® Publishing Association, Hagerstown, MD 21741-1119

All rights reserved. No portion of this book may be reproduced, stored in a retrieval system, or transmitted in any form or by any means (electronic, mechanical, photocopy, recording, scanning, or other), except for brief quotations in critical reviews or articles, without the prior written permission of the publisher.

Review and Herald® titles may be purchased in bulk for educational, business, fund-raising, or sales promotional use. For information, e-mail SpecialMarkets@reviewandherald.com.

The Review and Herald® Publishing Association publishes biblically based materials for spiritual, physical, and mental growth and Christian discipleship.

The author assumes full responsibility for the accuracy of all facts and quotations as cited in this book.

Texts credited to NIV are from the *Holy Bible, New International Version.* Copyright © 1973, 1978, 1984, 2011 by Biblica, Inc. Used by permission. All rights reserved worldwide.

This book was
Edited by Steve Chavez
Copyedited by Ted Hessel
Designed by Mark Bond
Typeset: Minion Pro 11/13

PRINTED IN U.S.A.

16 15 14 13 12   5 4 3 2 1

Library of Congress Cataloging-in-Publication Data
Beach, Bert Beverly.
  Ambassador for liberty : building bridges of faith, friendship, and freedom / Bert B. Beach.
    p. cm.
  1. Beach, Bert Beverly. 2. Seventh-Day Adventists—Biography. I. Title.
  BX6193.B43A3 2012
  286.2092—dc23
  [B]
                                        2012006021

ISBN 978-0-8280-2659-8

DEDICATION

This memoir is dedicated with gratitude to the three "families," from small to very large, that have had a significant impact on my life.

First, I mention my Beach family. It has given me a good name. I have traced this family tree back 10 generations, not a moral taint to be detected, but industrious individuals, true American pioneer stock, moving north and west, and on my mother's Corley side, south and west.

I'm grateful for a father and mother who were bright lights of inspiration in the home, and taught me the basic Christian truth: "Jesus loves me, this I know, for the Bible tells me so." They also encouraged me to plumb the depths of biblical thinking.

I appreciate having two loving and church-oriented sisters, with their successful offspring. I thank God for a devoted and intelligent Christian wife and two gifted Adventist daughters, of whom, with their spouses, I am proud; and the four grandchildren, who give us joy and are beginning to make their marks.

Second, my Seventh-day Adventist Church "family," the church of the remnant, which is very dear to me, and with which I have been identified all my life, have visited in about 140 countries, and will serve as long as service lasts.

Third, the Conference of Secretaries of Christian World Communions "family," representing close to 2 billion Christians, which I served as secretary for 32 years, and which widened my horizon and enlarged my vision of what it means to be a Christian.

APPRECIATION . . .

I owe a great debt of gratitude to my friend, Stephen Chavez, coordinating editor of *Adventist Review*. Without his optimism and helpful editorial mind and expertise, this project would very likely have been aborted and ended like a noncompleted Atlantic crossing or a truncated alpine tunnel-piercing. He swept me out of the navigation doldrums, and took me from the writing darkness to the light beckoning at the end of the tunnel. Thus, this work is partly his. While the story, concepts, words, and, likely, mistakes are all mine, the computer requirements and pragmatic outworkings are largely Steve's.

CONTENTS

Preface 11
Foreword: No One Could Replace You, Bert! 13
Introduction 15

Part I: Being
1 My First Glimpse of Life: The French Alps................19
2 The Church in Europe Reorganizes 22
3 Black Clouds Gather: The War Years 27
4 Life at Pacific Union College.......................................33
5 A Learning Experience 39
6 Postgraduate Work 41
7 Dr. Jean Nussbaum..45
8 Italy Calls 46
9 A Half-Century Love Story 51
10 Encouragement and Life Imprints 54
11 Speaking Well 61

Part II: Doing
12 Into Division Administration 67
13 An Observer to Vatican II 73
14 Early Travels for the Church 78
15 Life-altering Events 81
16 A Religious Liberty Lesson 84
17 Czechoslovakia: From Banned to Free.......................85
18 Travels in Africa 87
19 Speaking the Truth 103
20 Public Affairs and Religious Liberty—New Global Approach..106
21 Crisis in Nicaragua 108

22	Recognized by the United Nations	110
23	Papal Audiences	113
24	Calendar Reform	117
25	Interchurch Relations	120
26	A Half Century of Visits to Poland	125
27	Clubs and Associations—Unexpected Fallout	130
28	Writer *Malgré Lui*	135

Part III: Thinking

29	Bridge Building: A Life Work of Hope	141
30	The Adventist Christian and Politics	142
31	A Changing Church	144
32	Taking a Stand	146
33	Places and Events With Special Meaning	150
34	Random Experiences	152
35	Trust and True Unity	157
36	A Pilgrimage With Friends	159
37	Travel and Other Reflections	163
38	Money and Possessions	168
39	What a Universe! What a God! What Lessons!	170
40	The Revived Spiritual Life	176

Appendix

Honors and Distinctions 181

Index

.... 183

PREFACE

For several years various individuals have asked me to write my memoirs or autobiography. For a long time I resisted the temptation, for at least three reasons.

First, I knew it would involve a lot of work. After you retire, you do not have, and you miss, the splendid secretarial help you had while in office. I was blessed with such outstanding assistance for some 50 years. I suppose you get spoiled and used to having this support.

Second, I wondered how one went about writing such a personal book. It was a path on which I had never trod. Was there anything others might find interesting, even uplifting, in reading about me?

Third, in reading memoirs, I often felt that they tended to tell people how great the writer was and the wonderful things they had done, but glossed over other aspects of the life that would present a different picture. So I felt that it would be better to have some other person write a biography of me. A couple starts were actually made, but for different reasons they did not go far.

One day Steve Chavez told me rather firmly that *I* should write the book. He said people were not interested in knowing what *he* or *others* thought about me, but would much rather read what I had to say about the interesting life God had given me to live. Others supported his viewpoint. I tried to say no, but finally gave in and decided to bite the bullet. This book is the result.

Memoirs are a great thing, but memory can play tricks, especially when the passing of time or available publishing space forces certain parts of one's life to be reduced or left out entirely. However, for the author the memory still remains, albeit at times seen as through a glass darkly.

The first section of the book, which deals with being, or becoming, presents what happened in my life in a reasonably chronological order. The material in the other two sections—doing and thinking—present first activities, appointments, events, and finally my thoughts about life and the

Adventist Church in a more turning, circling, even jumping-around style. Many will remember that playing hopscotch as children was fun.

It's been a long life. I've been able to cover only a few things, events, and issues that reveal, I hope, some of the throb and thrust of the life God has blessed me with. If there have been a few successes, I thank my family and coworkers for making this possible. But the praise and any glory go to God, who covers our weaknesses, sees the end from the beginning, and "doeth all things well."

FOREWORD

No One Could Replace You, Bert!

It was one of my first visits to religious leaders with Bert Beach. I had just been nominated as General Conference director of the Public Affairs and Religious Liberty Department, a position that Bert had held for 15 years. As he introduced me as the one who had replaced him, one of the leaders smiled and said: "No one could replace you, Bert." It is so true! In many ways Bert is one of a kind.

It was a great honor, privilege, and blessing to have him as an advisor for a number of years after he retired. Bert introduced me to the top religious leaders in the world. He prepared me as his successor as secretary of the Conference of Secretaries of the Christian World Communions—a position he had occupied for 32 years.

No Seventh-day Adventist has ever had such influence or been more respected among top Christian leaders than Bert Beach. He represented the Adventist family with intelligence and courage in many international meetings. He presented an image of openness and seriousness without compromising his beliefs. He was proud of his church, without denigrating others. In official meetings Bert was often the one we asked to find the right word or to recall a historical reference.

I remember him standing at the conclusion of a dinner with government ministers, ambassadors, and religious leaders, speaking with authority and humor. His words were precise, his intelligence was *au rendez-vous*, and people were impressed. "Who is he?" some asked. The answer came very fast: "Beach!" At a dinner in London hosted by the archbishop of Canterbury, Bert thought he had the final word; but after his speech an Anglican priest offered a toast to "Bert Beach, the most High Church Adventist." This was—in the context of this dinner—a great compliment.

In meetings and dialogues in which we explain our beliefs, it sometimes happens that our position is not well understood. On occasion a heavy silence will fall on the room and the tension is strong. In those situations Bert has been the one to restore good relations by a few appropriate words or a bit of humor. He has made many friends over the years, and it has been for the good of his church.

As he gave a report on a dialogue to our Administrative Committee and read the final statement, someone suspiciously asked: "Where does this text come from?" It was not an easy moment. But Bert, with a smile, answered, "My brother, it comes directly from Mount Sinai!" Everyone laughed.

Bert Beach was also a great defender of religious freedom. Having him as speaker in a congress or a symposium was always a must. He spoke with passion, enthusiasm, and a great sense of logic and humor. His presence in a group of experts changed the atmosphere. He brought life and knowledge, passion and respect, competence and encouragement. Traveling with him, working with him, meeting with him, was an unforgettable experience. It was never boring.

Bert is unique, and he made a great difference in the church's history of relations with others. He opened new doors and built new bridges in such a way that it was a privilege for me to follow his path as he followed Jesus' path.

Like Bert, this book is unique. The reader will enjoy and absorb some of his exuberant energy, while also absorbing much information and learning life's lessons.

—**John Graz,** Director
Public Affairs and Religious Liberty
General Conference of Seventh-day Adventists

INTRODUCTION

God uses men and women in many ways, preparing them for future church work that will impact the proclamation of the three angels' messages of Revelation for these last days of earth's history as we look forward to Christ's soon coming. To study the lives of individuals brings out fascinating details of God's direct intervention in their lives.

Nancy and I have long been friends of Eliane and Bert Beach, as were my parents. As a young man, I looked up to and respected Bert's father, W. R. Beach, who was secretary of the General Conference for many years. Bert received a strong introduction to church work through the influence of his mother and father. Bert has been blessed with a creative and productive mind and an international perspective that have been useful in dealing with public and church activities. His life's linguistic and cultural backgrounds have been valuable assets in his work, writings, and the many international contacts he has made for the Adventist Church and its unique mission. He has contributed much to the world church through strong and consistent religious liberty and freedom of conscience work and advocacy in his capacity for many years as director of the Public Affairs and Religious Liberty Department of the General Conference of Seventh-day Adventists. He is an educator who has held strong interest in the development and promotion of a strong Seventh-day Adventist educational system. He also has had a strong influence on, and been a defender of, church policies and procedures to help the world church best accomplish its evangelistic mission.

I first met Bert in 1956 at the Italian Union Training School in Florence, Italy. This was during the Suez Crisis when I lived in Cairo, Egypt, as a young boy. When violence broke out and there was danger, my mother, my sister, and I as well as others were evacuated to Italy. My father stayed in Egypt during the crisis to continue nurturing the Seventh-day Adventist Church in that part of the Middle East. Bert was the principal of the Seventh-day Adventist college in Florence. After our brief stay at the college, we were instructed to proceed to Beirut, Lebanon, to wait until the crisis in Egypt calmed down. Bert drove us to the train station as we began our journey. While we were getting on the train, we discovered that one small bag was missing. Bert raced back to the parking lot outside the station, found the bag, and came running down the platform as the train started to pull out. He was able to thrust the missing bag to us through the door of the moving train. He has remained a good friend ever since that boyhood experience of rescuing our suitcase!

Bert's has been a long and very interesting life. As you read this book, you will catch a vivid glimpse of God's leadings and care that have helped build up the Adventist Church and its image in simple as well as exciting circumstances. You will meet interesting and dedicated people and will learn some of life's important lessons—the most important being complete trust in God's guidance and leading. You will gain knowledge and revived spiritual encouragement to face the climactic period of these decisive times as we see the prophecies of Daniel, Matthew, and Revelation being fulfilled and the final chapters of *The Great Controversy*, by Ellen G. White, unfolding before us.

You will gain a new appreciation for the need of guidance by the Holy Spirit in dealing with government and civic leaders in the very important and delicate areas of religious liberty and freedom of conscience as we base our beliefs completely on the Bible, God's Holy Word. You will respect even more our need for revival and reformation through the power of the Holy Spirit to help us rely totally on God's direction in fulfilling the important understanding that "the price of liberty is eternal vigilance." Certainly, as you read this book, you will understand better how God directs our personal lives and activities in helping us witness for Him and His biblical truth in unusual situations as we focus on Christ's soon second coming.

—**Ted N. C. Wilson,** President
General Conference of Seventh-day Adventists

PART I:
BEING

"Nothing is beneath the notice of the infinite God. . . . The Lord is constantly employed in upholding and using as His servants the things He has made."
—Ellen G. White, *Testimonies for the Church*, vol. 8, pp. 260, 261

"For in him we live, and move, and have our being" (Acts 17:28).

Chapter 1

MY FIRST GLIMPSE OF LIFE: THE FRENCH ALPS

I was born Bert Beverly Beach on a summer day in 1928 along the shores of Lake Geneva, at the then newly established Seventh-day Adventist Sanitarium, or *Clinique La Lignière*. Today it is a well-recognized medical center, where patients love to recover in the care of a first-rate medical staff, but it no longer does surgery or obstetrics. The room where I and my mother stayed after delivery faced Lake Geneva and Mount Blanc, the crown jewel of the French Alps and the highest mountain peak in western Europe. Years later as a young man, and even later as a grandfather, I gazed at this famous mountain and even hiked across its glacier, whispering to myself that I was born into a countryside of spectacular elevated beauty. Perhaps this earliest and continuing vision of beauty and altitude has silently encouraged me to climb the intricate heights of service and leadership.

Another Birth

As I reflect on my birth I am lured to think about my father, because his role in the drama of my life was paramount.

The circumstances of my birth were very different from those surrounding the birth of my father, Walter Raymond Beach. While I was born on a mild summer's day in what was known as ideal vacation territory, he was born in the midst of a snowstorm in January 1902, on a windswept homestead at St. John near the Turtle Mountains in North Dakota, a few miles from the Canadian border.

Whereas I was my parents' firstborn, my father was the lastborn, both of his parents being well into their 40s. The time of delivery came when the house and barn were buried in a snowdrift. Anxiety prevailed, and prayer was offered. How could the doctor and midwife get through? Suddenly they heard the music of tinkling bells. My grandfather Herbert, after whom I am named, opened the door, went outside, looked around, but saw no one. In extremely cold temperatures sounds can travel great distances; yet the family took this mysterious melody as a sign from God: heavenly music telling them, particularly the expectant mother whose time of delivery was a few hours away, not to worry or be afraid. The doctor and the midwife somehow got through. The child was born and dedicated to the Lord's work. He became a great preacher and inspiring leader in the Seventh-day Adventist Church.

Quo Vadis, Bert?

As far back as I can remember I understood that I would serve God and His church in one capacity or another, but the question was What type of service? My mother, Gladys, was a Texas girl of Baptist parents. She was sent to Laurelwood Academy and Walla Walla College by her Adventist aunt, Attie Chandler, who had moved to faraway Oregon and recognized Gladys' great potential. She met her future husband, my father, at that college, and after they were married they became longtime missionaries in Europe, concluding their service by working at the General Conference, where Walter was secretary for some 16 years.

My mother wanted me to become a missionary surgeon. A woman with a heightened sense of romance, she had read books about physicians achieving the stature of sainthood or miracle worker in the Belgian Congo and African bush, so she somehow fancied that I could add a new facet to the family gem by becoming a famous tropical doctor. By contrast, my dad once told me, I'm sure partly in jest, "Well, if you can't speak, write, or lead people, medicine might be OK!"

His aspirations were subtle but not hidden. He hoped I, his only son, would follow in his footsteps. Such expectations were not always easy to bear. I'm reminded of Winston Churchill's son, Randolph, who said that he often felt like a sapling living under the boughs of a great oak! In simple biblical terms: "To whom much is given, much will be required" (see Luke 12:48).

Europe Calls

In 1926 my parents accepted a call to serve as missionaries in Europe. Though my father had studied Spanish and expected to be sent to Spain, they were sent to Paris, France, where for a year my father studied French and French culture almost night and day at the Sorbonne (University of Paris). Knowing that the French were obsessively fussy about the pronunciation and use of their Gallic language—especially lampooning the English slaughter of the guttural French *r*—my father hired a retired French actress to coach him in mastering the pointed French vowels and the diabolic *r*. My mother has repeatedly described how my father would tirelessly trudge up and down the narrow hallway of their tiny flat at 130 Boulevard de l'Hospital, gargling gulps of water in order to master the rolling sound of that telltale consonant. The result, a year later, was that my father spoke French with barely a trace of the famous drawl with which most Americans give themselves away if they learned to speak French as adults.

Thus Paris and French culture left a deep imprint on my own life. Learning French as a small boy was a breeze. Instead of a language coach, all I needed were a few companions and my younger sister Jo Ray to master French as my mother tongue.

But I am getting ahead of my story.

Chapter 2

THE CHURCH IN EUROPE REORGANIZES

In 1928, the year I was born, the church decided to split the European Division into three divisions: the Northern European Division, with headquarters in England; the Southern European Division, taking over the office in Bern that had been the division office for all of Europe; and the Central European Division, which consisted of Germany, Austria, Czechoslovakia, Hungary, and the Netherlands. It also had some mission territories in the former German colonies in Africa and the Dutch colony of what is now Indonesia.

My father was youth and education director at the old Latin Union Conference, with headquarters in Gland, Switzerland, where I was born. He was 26, and it was felt he wasn't quite ready yet to work at the division level, so when the Latin Union was disbanded, church leaders asked him to be president of the Belgian Conference. Thus, we lived in Belgium from 1929 to 1932. My sister Joyce Raymonde (later called Jo Ray) was born here, which forced my mother to divide her attention between two babies. I have been told that I revealed in some infantile ways that my nose was out of joint because I now was no longer sole ruler of the domain of children. Doggedly thumping my head on the floor was one such notice—a rather ironic gesture considering the close bond Jo Ray and I have shared all our lives.

I remember very little about these Belgian childhood years, but they were doubtless of great importance in my life, as the reader will see.

I remember one somewhat amusing experience in Brussels: My parents had some guests, and I was sent to my room. I obviously didn't like this. Sometime later a police officer rang the bell and told my parents that a small boy was shoving shoes from a bedroom window to the sidewalk below. I don't remember what happened to me, but I do know I never did it again.

Another childish act took place at the Belgian seaside where my mother took us for a couple weeks in the summer. There was a tram, or streetcar, that plied the coast between beach resorts. I enjoyed hearing the conductor blow his whistle, to communicate to the driver that they were ready to go. I got my parents to buy me a whistle that I chose because of its "train sound." In due course I used it near the tram. Sure enough, the tram took off lickety-split! I seem to recall that my mother, like England's Queen Victoria, "was not amused."

After living in Belgium for three years, my father became president of the Franco-Belgian Union in Paris. So we lived in Paris from 1932 to 1936 in an apartment on the floor above the union conference office. Today the apartment is part of the North France Conference, and the union conference office is located a distance outside Paris.

When my father arrived in Paris, the church wanted him to learn French and understand French culture. So he went to the University of Paris and took language studies. A voracious reader, he devoured Descartes, Racine, Moliere, and Hugo in addition to the best French theologians. He was intrigued by the growing debate concerning the historical Jesus taking place at that time among theologians in France and Germany. After poring over Joseph Ernest Renan's famous *Vie de Jesus* and the scholarly responses it elicited, he finally agreed with Albert Schweitzer, who, after studying Renan, insisted that all of the popular studies of the historical Jesus said more about the beliefs of the authors than about the life of Jesus.

My father learned French exceedingly well. In fact, he wrote books in French, not translated from English. When he died, there was an obituary, written by Jean Zurcher, secretary of the Euro-Africa Division, that included these words: "He even spoke an elegant French."

In France word got around that my father was really French. Native French who heard him speak might think, *Well, he's not from our little town; he's most likely from 100 kilometers away, where they speak with his intonation.* Southern France has an intonation as different to a person from northern France as the Southern drawl in the United States sounds to someone's ear in New England.

Christian Education—A Limited View

I started first grade in Paris, at a school within walking distance of our home. A few years ago I visited the building. It was no longer being used as a school, but as state education administration offices. The two entrance doors still had, etched in stone, the words *"garcons"* on one and *"filles"* on the other, indicating the former separation of the sexes.

The Seventh-day Adventist work in Europe started with many great Christian disciples—energetic and dedicated. L. R. Conradi was an early gifted promoter and energizer, who eventually became president of the European Division, but, unfortunately, left the church late in his life. He, as others, saw Christian education more as a seminary that prepared workers for the church—ministers, secretaries, accountants, and business managers. He and other leaders somewhat ignored elementary and secondary education, thinking that the government was taking care of those segments admirably with taxes, so why should the church pay for a duplicate school? That restrictive approach and outlook have never been completely vanquished in Europe, though progress has been made. Some areas did support Adventist schools, the most successful being the Nordic countries of Denmark, Norway, Sweden, and Finland. In England they had church schools, but not many. One or two existed in Switzerland, but most countries had none.

I laughingly tell people that my career path was well prepared while I was a boy in Bern, the capital of Switzerland, where my parents moved in 1936, which I will explain later. My mother was a superb and generous host to any of the "brethren" who used Bern as part of their travel route. I drank and ate with church administrators, departmental directors, teachers, or pastors a good share of each month, particularly before the war. The pastors and administrators came through regularly; I met them all. In those days our people didn't often eat at restaurants; such a habit was probably considered wasteful, maybe even "sinful." So they came to homes and were entertained by local members.

I met many leaders and became interested in church work. I found it fascinating to hear conflicting views on the sanctuary question, or on how to formulate a budget and distribute the money, or who would be the best replacement for brother so-and-so's position in such-and-such a conference. Some people vexedly call these conversations "the politics of the church," but I always saw them as practical workshops to advance "the work."

My parents took it for granted that I would be a worker in the church. Nobody exactly used the word "pastor," but how do you get to be a successful voice or force in the church without being some kind of pastor?

My mother continued to hint that I should be a missionary doctor somewhere, maybe like Livingstone or Schweitzer in Africa. She gave me books to read, biographies of some of these great people. I liked reading them. But when I went to school, I didn't take to some subjects that were connected with what might be called "premedical."

I think I would have enjoyed medicine in terms of helping people, but not dealing with medications, memorizing bones, muscles, and nerves of the body. I was interested in history, geography, sociology, theology, and philosophy.

Because of the Sabbath, I attended a private Presbyterian (Reformed) Church-related school in Bern for middle and high school. State schools required class attendance on Saturdays, imposing strict truancy laws that occasionally went as far as fines or placing Adventist parents in prison if they did not see to it that their offspring attended school on Saturday. Unlike public schools, private schools in the canton of Bern were free to give Sabbath privileges. Like some other Adventist expatriates before us, my parents enrolled us in the prestigious Freies Gymnasium of Bern. As a result, I received the best education available and associated with students from good families. But private school was expensive, and my parents had to make financial sacrifices to pay for my tuition and that of my two sisters.

While in the Freies Gymnasium high school, I was, until my last year, an average student. After all, I missed classroom activities one day out of six. Then, too, I liked extracurricular activities, such as sports, reading, and school fraternity. In short, I confess I didn't study enough! I did catch up at the end and went on to college and university and got good grades. Unlike me, my wife was a diligent student, always first or second in her class. Thus both of our daughters did well in their studies; my wife saw to that!

Early in school in Bern I learned several lessons. The first was honesty. I greatly disliked art, or "drawing" as it was called; probably because I found the teacher surly and incompetent as a teacher. One day he assigned us as homework to paint an apple in gray. One of my classmates, Esther Stein (a friend of Jo Ray's), was gifted in art and came to our home after school. When I complained about the assignment, she offered to help me. In fact, she did most of the drawing and watercolor. I felt happy to submit such a fine piece of homework. However, the teacher easily detected my ruse, and as a result I was forced to have a short but embarrassing conversation with the school principal. Since I was the only Adventist in my class, I felt I had betrayed my religious principles and vowed to maintain a high standard of integrity in the future.

I remember another lesson that later came in handy in my job as an educator. While in the sixth grade I was failing math. The teacher, Samuel Gmünder, told us one day, "Several of you are failing or struggling in math. I am willing to give you private tutoring for an hour after school." He brought me up to par in a few weeks. In fact, from then on I became a good math student on my own. I remember this teacher with respect and gratitude; he taught me how important it is for teachers to be interested in the success of their students, and be willing to go the extra mile to help them.

Sound Religion at Home

I was fortunate to grow up in a home where my parents were staunch, 100 percent Seventh-day Adventists. But they weren't fanatical, with closed minds—focusing in a persnickety way on "what you don't eat" or "where you don't go" as the true emblem of being a good Seventh-day Adventist. My parents brought their children up to believe that diet is a matter of health, not a matter of taboos. I've had people tell me, "I'd rather die than eat meat." Well, if people tell you that, it means they don't understand health reform. Health reform is healthful *living*; it's not *dying*. You try to eat the best you can under the circumstances.

So we didn't have a fanatical atmosphere in the home. My father was an intellectual, a thinker, but not dry or morbid. He was uplifting in the home, in the office, in the pulpit, and in the church. I hope some of that divine gift rubbed off on me. As a wise student of mine in Italy once told me: "One can always try hope."

Chapter 3

BLACK CLOUDS GATHER: THE WAR YEARS

When I was young, any family transferred by the General Conference to mission service in Europe faced a 10-year assignment. After 10 years they earned a furlough, but not before. Today some pundits might consider this "cruel and unusual punishment," perhaps even prohibited by the U.S. Constitution (just kidding)!

The sacrifices made by missionary families are multiple and rarely fully understood by people who consider only the glamour of living in an alluring foreign land, full of brilliant opportunities for travel, cultural enrichment, and helping the less fortunate. Consider, for example, that my sisters and I *never* had the privilege of seeing grandparents, uncles, aunts, and cousins at any time while we were living abroad.

When one of my Swiss friends explained that he couldn't play soccer with me on Wednesday because that was the day he was invited to visit with his grandmother, I always felt a twinge of envy. Even as I watched arguments among cousins, I felt that somehow I was missing out on unique ties and encounters. I saw my father's mother only once, and I saw the other three grandparents rarely and only fleetingly. I was 8 years old before I ever set foot on American soil to meet relatives and to participate in typical American customs.

A Front-Row Seat to War

The United States went to war in 1941. But for me World War II had started in 1939. The first thing I did at my high school in Bern after the U.S. entered the war was to organize an "Anti-Axis Club."

Switzerland was caught in an intricate political situation: In 1940 it was a small country with a little more than 4 million citizens surrounded by Nazi-occupied countries. Switzerland had to import most of its food and fuel. Fortunately, the Swiss equivalent of what we might call the Department of Agriculture, but with more power, had foreseen the situation and had accumulated a lot of food. So when the war broke out in

September 1939, the Swiss government immediately rationed all food, and for a time our rations were smaller than those in France or Germany. One good aspect about the Swiss situation was that you could buy whatever you had on your ration tickets when you went to the store; the store had it in stock.

My father had read that in wartime a smart preventive measure was to stock up on soap so you could avoid diseases spread by filthy sanitation. He also felt that the famous Swiss Toblerone triangular chocolate bars contained excellent food supplements, so he stocked up on soap and chocolate. Mother stocked up on cans including Nestle's sweetened condensed milk. Anyone with a modicum of imagination can visualize the Beach children sneaking into our pantry when no one was looking to gobble up a piece of chocolate or to steal a sip of condensed milk. Jo Ray remembers that we used to barter our rations with each other and with friends in the neighborhood. "I'll give you a piece of Toblerone if you give me a slice of ginger *broetli*."

My wife, Eliane, grew up in occupied Belgium during the war. There, you had ration tickets saying, for example, that you could get 100 grams of butter—but you had to find a store that had butter. If you couldn't—which became more and more the case—you had to go to the black market, where you might be able to find needed food at an inflated price, paying four or five times more than usual. There was no black market in Switzerland, where the Swiss reputation for honor and fairness would have shuddered at black market dealings.

We thanked God that we had canned goods. We could use powdered eggs to make omelets. My mother also learned to use potato flour to make sauces and cakes. Her enormous culinary talents enhanced our wartime menus so that we never really suffered. My sisters and I remember with fondness a particular chocolate pudding she created out of cocoa, powdered eggs, very little sugar, milk, and potato flour. Refrigeration then was not what it is now. Because we didn't have a refrigerator in our home, much of the year we just placed food outside on our balcony to keep it cool. Residents in our apartment house had access to a food cellar, where we kept crisp apples and potatoes from nearby farms all through the war.

Coal too was heavily rationed. I was the official coal boy in our family, so it was my duty to climb down to the coal bin in the cellar and bring up the coal and start the heat every morning. Since coal was very scarce, we also used peat, cut from the ground in the form of bricks. My mother claimed that I grumbled about that duty most mornings. "Why do I have to have the worst job in the family?" I would mutter. As I recall, we never suffered a dangerous illness during the freezing Swiss winter snowstorms, but my mother longed for the warm weather of her Texas hometown and often lived with her back pressed against the radiator of our living room.

From 1939 to 1940 my father could travel because the Swiss borders with France and Italy were still open. The Germans hadn't occupied France yet. The war raged more on the border between France and Germany. Instead of striking France, the Germans went through Belgium, around the Maginot line, and through the Netherlands. They had armored tank divisions and an air force, all ready for the blitzkrieg. The French weren't as well equipped. So when the Germans marched into France, the French army collapsed.

Ordered Home

With the fall of France, the American consul in Bern told my parents, "You have to go home." The division office in England closed during the war. A lot of Americans were on the division staff near London. That was clearly a war situation; they were being bombed. I think some of the Americans were happy to get out.

A. V. Olson, president of the Southern European Division, and my father, secretary of the division, decided to stay in Switzerland, despite orders from the U.S. Embassy, and try to keep the division office and work going as normally as possible and not abandon ship and return to the United States. God's protecting hand rested on us and the church in Switzerland all during the war. We suffered no casualties or invasions.

In Switzerland we were fortunate. Germany had invaded other countries, but it did not invade Switzerland. It was probably in its own self-interest. What would be obtained by invading Switzerland? It had very few natural resources, no oil. In those days the Swiss were passionately nationalistic and patriotic. They were convinced that if the Germans came, they'd show them. "They'll lose a million men!"

In fact, several times during the war the Swiss government proclaimed "general mobilization," and within a few hours every able Swiss adult male arrived at his assigned post, ready to defend his country. There is no doubt that if attacked and invaded, they would have fought from the réduit, the redoubt fortifications tunneled within the Alps. They were ready.

For self-protection, the Swiss were forced to implement blackouts demanded by Germany; they were also forced to shoot at American and British planes that flew over Switzerland. The allies flew over Switzerland to go to Germany, Italy, or Austria. The Swiss would shoot at them, but I never heard of a plane being shot down. It was nevertheless scary, because you'd hear BOOM, BOOM, BOOM, and because the roofs in Bern were made of tiles, hearing the noise of shrapnel bouncing on roofs was alarming. I remember clearly one evening, when my parents were away, my little sister, Colette, came into my room crying, wanting to sleep near me because she was terrified of the noise and filled with panic.

As a youth I saw the war as my father did: pro-France, pro-Belgium, pro-Britain, pro-Allies, anti-Nazis. After all, France was the country of Lafayette, and in World War I we had been together against the kaiser.

Prophecies and Newspaper Headlines

Some Adventists saw Hitler the way they had viewed the kaiser during World War I—as some kind of fulfillment of biblical prophecy. But it is always dangerous to get too prophetic about matters announced in newspapers or radio headlines. You have to *wait*, let the smoke clear and the dust settle, and get a fuller and more reliable and enduring picture before you make prophetic assessments. Not every evil or controversial person looms in history as a distinctive prophetic figure. Sometimes an oppressor is just that—an oppressor, and nothing more.

War Games

In the evenings my father and I sat by the radio listening to the Swiss Broadcasting Network. Swiss radio tried to be neutral. It would blare out over the radio waves, "According to reports from Berlin . . . "; "The BBC has announced . . . "; "Washington says . . . " So they would give both sides of the story. After all, the Swiss neutrality had been generally recognized in international law since the Congress of Vienna in 1815.

Listening to the British Broadcasting Corporation, when possible, was a ritual my father and I observed with growing suspense. The Germans would jam the signals, but the BBC broadcasted over five or more different channels, and we could usually hear one. We couldn't hear Voice of America too well, since that was shortwave. My father and I unfolded a big map of Europe and placed it on a table in front of us. We planted different-colored pins on it to show exactly which position the different armies had reached. For me, sitting evenings in front of that map with my father was like playing the most fascinating game imaginable. During those moments I ignored my sisters and anyone else who tried to divert my attention from the private war game that absorbed me at a crucial time in European history.

Closed Borders

The church's division office in Bern functioned fully until 1940, when the Germans swept into France. But the offices continued to operate in a limited capacity in France, Belgium, Spain, Portugal, and Italy. Until the middle of 1940 my father could travel by train to Italy. In fact, Italians never did like the idea of fighting Americans, because they had families in America. I'm told that there were more Italians in New York than there were in Rome at the time. They were anti-Britain, because of the colonial situation. But America was not a colonial power.

When Italy entered the war, the Italian border was closed; when the Germans occupied France, the French border was closed. And from December 1941, when war broke out between Germany and the United States, there was no way of getting out of Switzerland at all. So from 1941 to late 1944 the division office functioned, but it was by mail and by heroic couriers like John Weidner, who crossed borders secretly at Collonges or elsewhere, bringing strategic correspondence. In sum, the borders were not 100 percent tight. Diplomats could travel, and some of our mail would arrive by way of diplomatic pouches. So the division office did function, with limitations.

When my father could no longer travel outside Switzerland, he became editor of the French *Life and Health* magazine, which was printed in Switzerland. Somehow it got out of Switzerland and was distributed in other European countries. I don't know how exactly it crossed the border.

Helping Swiss Radio

Then the Swiss Broadcasting Corporation (SBC) asked my father if he would be willing to help them. So my father worked for the SBC in the evenings. He was a speaker for the news on shortwave. They were beaming news to America because many American Swiss liked to hear the news from Switzerland. No television existed in those days. These SBC newscasts were in English, and very few English-speaking people were left in Switzerland, particularly with an American accent. All had left. My father and my mother worked for the SBC for a couple years. My mother even prepared children's programs that were beamed to America. She would tell stories of Swiss heroes and legends—William Tell and all that. My mother was a good writer and storyteller; she had that gift. Their work was really esteemed. I worked at the SBC myself for several weeks to help out. But I didn't stay long; I was too young, around 16 or 17. My voice hadn't quite matured yet. My English wasn't that good either.

The war ended for us with a great triumph. I still remember Churchill's thrilling but matter-of-fact speech when he announced the end of the war in Europe. He concluded by saying, "Advance, Britannia!" and "God save the king!"

I also remember listening to Hitler, since German radio was easy to get. No more than 30 days before his death in his Berlin bunker, Hitler proclaimed (in German, of course), "England will go down; but Germany is going forward toward a thousand-year empire." He was deluded, to put it mildly. The Russians were entering Berlin. The Allies had crossed the Rhine and Elbe on the other side. It was finished. For us the war was largely over. Japan was on the other side of the globe. God had protected His church, and us. How thankful we were.

Chapter 4

LIFE AT PACIFIC UNION COLLEGE

After the end of the war in 1945, it was time to think about a college education for my sister Jo Ray and me. My father had graduated from Walla Walla College. He knew Percy Christian, who later became president of Pacific Union College (PUC). PUC was situated on a crest of Howell Mountain, up in the hills above St. Helena in California's lovely Napa Valley. Since Jo Ray and I had spent most of our lives in Switzerland, a country that was mountainous, full of green meadows, and famous for its luxuriant woods, my parents felt that by going to college at PUC, Jo Ray and I would be in a more familiar atmosphere, where we would feel comfortable and less homesick. I had never been away from my mother for more than two weeks. Then suddenly I was separated from her by a continent and the Atlantic Ocean, forced to communicate only by torturously slow letters, not by telephone (too costly) or the instant e-mail students use today.

A Special Friend

The only person I knew at PUC when I arrived in the summer of 1946 was John Tarr, the son of A. F. Tarr. We had met a few weeks earlier at a General Conference (GC) session held in the Sligo church in Takoma Park, Maryland. In those days we were still able to have a "plenipotentiary" General Conference session in the Sligo church—except for Sabbath, when we assembled in the Washington, D.C., Armory so that all delegates and guests could be seated.

John had come from India, a far different part of the world from the one in which I had been reared. Yet we had much in common and became instant friends. His father was secretary of the Southern Asia Division, and my father was secretary of the Southern European Division. Soon our fathers both became division presidents. John had a brilliant mind, and we were both fascinated by world events and theological ideas. John and I have remained close friends to this day. Even if we haven't seen each other for a long stretch of time, when we do meet we pick up our friendship as if no time had elapsed.

My first year at PUC I was assigned to a room in Grainger Hall with two nice fellows, Don Moran and Bill Haynes, who were young like me. Although I was a junior and they were freshmen, we got along well. They both later served the church in California.

Settling on a major was a troublesome choice for me. On one hand, I honored the ministry as all good Seventh-day Adventists; on the other hand, teaching and medicine were also venerated. I finally registered with a history major because I wanted to go on and do graduate work. In those days there wasn't much graduate work within the church available in theology. We had no seminary, but it would soon begin. You couldn't get a doctor's degree in Seventh-day Adventist schools except in medicine. I planned to go into the ministry, but not necessarily as a local pastor; maybe in education or departmental work. These, however, are not jobs to which you clearly aspire, or for which you signal your desire; you have to feel your way so as to fit the need and be selected.

A Bit Naive

I was at PUC until 1948. It was an interesting and instructive experience for me, because I was naive and uninitiated in American tradition or folklore. One night at full moon a group of mischievous male students invited me to what they termed "an exciting American custom—snipe hunting." Since I had come over from Europe and had never been to an American high school, these fellows thought, *Let's have a bit of fun with this guy from overseas.* So they took me out snipe hunting.

We left in one car with about six people in it. They'd drop one off, then another, and finally when they got to the farthest spot they announced, "The snipes are about ready to come." Then the car disappeared; I was left there in the middle of a dark forest alone. It took me 15 or 20 minutes before I figured out, *Something's going on here!* Being new at the school, I didn't even know where I was. Eventually I found my way back to the dormitory through the back entrance, too proud to admit that I had been had and even scared, but wiser for the experience.

My sister Jo Ray, however, did not let the matter drop. The next morning, when she found out what had happened, she confronted the ringleader with red-hot fury, looking him straight in the eye and yelling, "How dare you treat my brother in such a cavalier way! He could've been hurt. You and your buddies deserve permanent expulsion from college!" I was embarrassed by Jo Ray's outburst, but loyalty is deeply embedded in the Beach family. My hope was that the incident would soon die away and be forgotten, which it was.

I didn't know much about dating, but my friend George Harding did. He was John Tarr's roommate and a gifted student leader, with an interesting denominational and political background. One of his great-uncles was president of the United States (Warren G. Harding), and the other was religious liberty director of the General Conference (Heber Votaw). George's father was a Christian gentleman. A respected psychiatrist, he served for a time as president of the College of Medical Evangelists, now Loma Linda University. George and I have remained very close friends.

Watching George confidently approach a girl to ask her for a date served as a model for me, although I never came close to his easy style. There was a lot of competition for dates in those years, because the World War II veterans were coming back to college with their GI Bill of Rights. They weren't 18, 19, or 20; they were 24, 25, 26, and 27. They had cars, money, and maturity. I remember one of them, Marvin Fehrenbach, owned a jeep. How excited I was when on occasion he let me drive it on campus! I had lived in Bern during the war years, when nobody drove a car. There was no gas! Until well after the war my parents in Europe never owned a car.

A Spiritual Climate

I enjoyed the spiritual climate at PUC. It was conservative. The girls had to have their dresses a certain length. The preceptors would measure their hems when they dressed for a date or a reception. But there were events you could go to with girls. Although there were no major restrictions on seeing them, high standards of decorum were expected. The librarian once scolded me in the library because I was talking to a girl in the stacks. She later apologized, because someone had enlightened her that I was talking to Jo Ray.

I particularly esteemed Mark Hamilton, chair of the History Department, who later became a predecessor of mine in the Northern European Division, where John Tarr's father served as president. I recommended Hamilton to be educational director of the division. A respected gentleman, Hamilton had a Ph.D., a degree highly valued in those days because it was still a relatively rare attainment. On the campus at PUC I noticed two kinds of teachers—the same as I found at Columbia Union College, where I later taught for two years. There were those who were Doctor So-and-so and those who were Professor So-and-so. If you had a doctoral degree, you were called "Doctor"; if not, you were called "Professor." Today that distinction is no longer used in the same way.

In France and Germany and other countries in Europe, the title "professor" was, and still is, more prestigious than "doctor," because there a professor always has a doctorate. But not every doctor is a professor. Even today in many European countries, the title "professor" is an appointment made by the state, and is different from "doctor," which is usually a university degree.

I was president of the Foreign Mission Band at PUC. Today such an appointment would probably be less important than it was then—I am sorry to say; but in those days we had a Friday evening program every month or so to promote foreign missions. We discussed missions a lot; it seemed as though everyone talked about going to the mission field as a missionary for several years, not just for the summer. In fact, at every alumni homecoming at PUC (I don't know if they still do this) they would display the lighted missionary map, where every missionary from PUC had a little light. Some of the most charming and colorful entertainment on campus included missionary pageants that featured exotic costumes or music from such places as Australia, China, Japan, India, and Africa. When the colorful presentations from Hawaii became repetitive, we students loved to exclaim, with an edge of satire, "Well, today we listened to another delegation from Paradise." In general we enjoyed learning about incidents of strong faith in distant places. We caught a vision of what the apostles meant when they advocated preaching the gospel to the ends of the earth. Since leaving PUC I have been, almost literally, to the ends of the earth. The "eternal gospel" marches on.

While going to PUC I earned some extra money by working as a reader for the History Department. Earlier, when I first arrived on campus, I had worked for a short time in the fields landscaping. This job was not something I found inspiring! You have to remember that when I went to the gymnasium in Europe—and I'm talking about the 1930s and 1940s—gymnasium students did not do physical labor; that was for another class of people. None of the students at my school in Bern did any such work that I know of. Of course, that was a wrong concept.

Class System
All over Europe—Switzerland included—a strict class system existed. In other words, what you did for a living—working a trade or being a professional—was determined by your schooling. If you went to secondary school, you became a plumber, a carpenter, or some other trade. If you went to the gymnasium, you most likely continued on to the university and became a lawyer, doctor, or other profession. If you didn't go to the gymnasium, or lycée, it was almost impossible to get into the university. You might be able

later on to take some special examination. If you were truly gifted, an academic official might be able to help you somehow get in. But basically it was already decided by the time you were 11 or 12 years old whether you would be a doctor, lawyer, teacher, or exercise one of the trades.

My father, with his Jeffersonian view of equality, always protested the European system of locking out talented youth from receiving a higher education just because they belonged to a certain social class. He cited the example of my close friend Eugen Gafner, who, despite his obvious literary talents and insights, could hardly be anything but the owner of a nursery or gardening service because that was what his father had been. Fortunately for him, several years later, because of a shortage of teachers in the canton of Bern, a door opened for him to become a teacher.

A College "Fraternity"

While at PUC I belonged to a close-knit group of less than a dozen ambitious friends. We called it the "4:00 a.m. Club." Not that we got up at 4:00 in the morning, but that on occasion we went to bed at that time.

Most of our group was involved in putting out the *Campus Chronicle* (the PUC newspaper) and the *Diogenes Lantern* (the college yearbook). The founders were Ralph Jones (the most popular student on campus), George Harding, John Tarr, John Koning, James Parsons, and I. Richard Duncan and David Cotton also became members. Every one of these students went on to have successful careers. Most became outstanding doctors, and Ralph Jones a lawyer and judge in Walla Walla, Washington. Jim Parsons became a well-known political figure and psychologist in Anchorage, Alaska. Unfortunately, Ralph died young because of cancer. However, his wife, Pat, and his daughters are still friends.

Three faculty were members: Harold T. Jones, and the two most popular teachers on campus, George Meldrum and Joseph Fallon.

This group came the closest to being a sort of European-style college fraternity, binding us together for life and work. They served the church in some capacity or other.

The Halverson Connection

After I graduated from PUC, I went to work for the California Public Health Department. I got that summer job because the director of public health, Wilton L. Halverson, was a shirttail relative. The state capital was Sacramento, but for some reason the Health Department was in San Francisco.

Halverson and his wife, Hazel, took a special interest in Jo Ray and me. He was professor of public health at the University of California and the same at the College of Medical Evangelists, now Loma Linda University. He had been dean of boys at one of our academies. To my youthful eyes, Halverson was bigger than life and extremely important because he had been appointed by Earl Warren, then governor of California, to be director of public health for the state.

After he became chief justice of the U.S. Supreme Court, Warren wrote in his autobiography that when he was elected governor, he asked, "Now, who is the best man I can find to be director of the health department for the state?" He was told, "The best man you can find is the director of public health for the city of Pasadena." Halverson had a doctorate in public health from Yale and a medical degree from Loma Linda. He introduced me to Governor Warren and whetted my youthful appetite and interest in government and public affairs. The Halversons were very important to Jo Ray and me, and later Colette, during our PUC years and after. They gave us a home away from home. We were very close. Hazel lived past 100 years of age and was like a second mother to me. I had the honor of conducting her funeral at Loma Linda. Wilton died much earlier, while I was serving the church in Europe. I still remember with great pleasure several trips I took with Hazel in Europe, especially Scotland and northern Finland to see the midnight arctic sun.

I was still very young when I graduated from Pacific Union College in 1948. Looking back, I think it would have been good if I had stayed on another year. I graduated before my twentieth birthday.

Stanford Beckons

In the History Department at Pacific Union College we had two teachers, Mark Hamilton and George Meldrum, who had both earned their Ph.D.s from Stanford University. They counseled me to go to Stanford University for graduate work. I'm not sure I even knew Stanford existed before I went to PUC. So it wasn't clear to me exactly what university I should choose, but my father and I decided that a doctoral degree in history would be useful in my future educational career, whatever it might be. History touches upon so many aspects of society. In the end, I opted for Stanford, a decision I have never regretted.

At Stanford I expected eventually to go back to Europe. I knew French, German, and the Swiss German dialect. But when I finally returned to Europe in 1951, the church did as the U.S. Army used to do: It sent me to Italy in 1952, where I did not know the language at all. In the army, I'm told, if you're a cook you may become a driver; if you're a truck driver they'll put you in as a painter. I suppose this way they can train you as they wish!

Chapter 5

A LEARNING EXPERIENCE

My parents paid for me to get my B.A. at Pacific Union College, and they were helping me go on to Stanford University. So I worked a summer at the California Department of Public Health in San Francisco. I saved enough money to pay most of the tuition at Stanford, which cost $200 a quarter! Today this seems almost miraculous.

After a year of graduate work at Stanford, I decided I needed a regular job so that I could earn some money to continue my studies.

I was offered a job as principal of the Seventh-day Adventist school in Gridley, California, north of Sacramento and south of Chico. I don't know how I got that job. I didn't know anybody. I was probably on a list of PUC graduates who were thought to be available.

Mildred Ostich from the Northern California Conference Education Department approached me and asked if I'd be willing to do it. I wasn't especially interested in the place; I'd never even heard of Gridley before. But it was a starting point, and she was supportive, and knew my parents.

I became principal of West Liberty Union School. It served the churches of Gridley and Oroville, an intermediate school with 50 or 60 students, three full-time teachers, and two or three part-time teachers. It went to tenth grade. I taught grades 7, 8, 9, and 10. I taught everything except music. I don't think I was a very good teacher; I was learning myself. I'd never been to an American grade school or high school, and I went in as principal. Today the school has moved and is now called Feather River Adventist School.

One of the teachers, a much more experienced teacher, had been principal the previous year. But for some reason the board didn't want him to be principal that year; they wanted a change. He probably had a B.A., but I don't think he had any graduate work. They'd apparently heard that I'd been studying at Stanford, a young, eager guy. I was happy to hear that he returned as principal after I left.

The Gridley experience was a maturing and strengthening one. I was not a great teacher, but I learned pretty fast.

The stay at Gridley also gave me the opportunity to develop my preaching skills. I'm grateful for the confidence of the local pastor, Robert Thompson, and the local church members. They helped launch both my teaching and my preaching careers. I still remember a member who somehow felt he was an authority because he had some relative who had a leadership position in the denomination. After my first sermon in Gridley, he came up to me: "Young man, you still have a long way to go."

That was quite true, but was that the way to encourage a young person?

After the next sermon he said, "Young man, you did better today." It was good to know that I was not beyond the pale of hope! I must not have done too badly; the church ordained me as a local elder. I was then a ripe 21.

In 1950 I took two Cady brothers without charge into my large room where I was boarding with the friendly Sudduth family at the end of the school bus line. I also drove the school bus for $20 a month. The Cady brothers had lost their mother and needed help and a place to stay. I was happy to help, and after I left I lost track of them.

Fifty years later I preached in the Chico church (about 20 miles from Gridley), and these two Cady boys, now in their 60s, came up to me and introduced themselves. How pleased I was that they had done well. One was retired and the other had his own business as a laboratory technician. To top it all off, the pastor of the Chico church (in his 40s) was the son of one of the two! "All begins well that ends well!"

But it is a little worrisome to think that I had reached the precarious age when my students have middle-age children!

I met some very nice people in Gridley. It was a good experience for me.

Chapter 6

POSTGRADUATE WORK

I was happy after a year teaching school in Gridley, but I thought, *You have some experience now; it might be time to go back to school.* I intended to go back to Stanford, but I didn't have quite enough money. So I decided to go to the University of California at Berkeley for one year. However, because of a complication with credits, I went back to Stanford after one semester.

You could study at Stanford for your Ph.D. without an M.A., as long as you did the required courses and took the examinations. So at Stanford I was a Ph.D. candidate—at least I was heading in that direction. In order to get the M.A., I would have to do a thesis.

Looking back, I made a poor choice of topics. My father had always been interested in the French Revolution. And I was interested in it too; I had lived in Paris as a kid for three years, and later for 10 years in Bern. So my idea was to write a thesis on the influences of the French Revolution in Switzerland. Actually, that's a much too broad topic for a M.A. thesis, so I shouldn't have chosen it. Also, I found very little documentation in the library in Stanford on the subject. For an M.A. thesis you don't go wandering around the world. Who would pay for me to go to the Library of Congress or maybe Switzerland to do research? So I did some research, made a few notes, but then put the proposal on the back burner and started taking courses for my Ph.D.

I went one year at Stanford, one semester at Berkeley, and then one more quarter at Stanford. My experience in Berkeley had some important future fallout for me. I believe that in all this God was leading. I was active in the Berkeley church, as I was much later in the St. Albans (England) church. I made some good friends who left an imprint of lasting memories.

I became acquainted at Berkeley with a student who had obtained a doctorate from Paris. He gave me pointers and the name of a professor there to contact.

I took a course at Berkeley from Kenneth Stampp, a leading expert on the U.S. Civil War and Reconstruction period. He got me interested in that period of U.S. history. The Reconstruction period later became the topic of my doctoral dissertation. (When Stampp died in 2009 it caught the attention of the nation's press in the United States.)

Then I was called to go to Paris to be a part of the team of Jean Nussbaum, who was the most famous religious liberty man in the Southern European Division, and indeed, the Adventist world. He was also an evangelist.

Arriving in Paris the fall of 1951, I met the professor I was to contact, but since I was interested in French-American diplomatic relations, he told me the professor I needed to see was Pierre Renouvin, the leading French expert. I had read one of his books while I was at Stanford. Renouvin received me kindly and said he was willing to supervise my doctoral dissertation, but not on the U.S. Civil War, because, he said, this had been quite fully covered. He suggested I study the period of Reconstruction after the Civil War from the viewpoint of the French diplomats in the United States. It was providential that he accepted me, an unknown American student with—for a famous University of Paris scholar, no doubt—a strange religion! He was the leading French historian, chair of the department, editor of the *French Historical Review*, and a member of the prestigious Institute of France. He introduced me to the French Foreign Ministry at the Quai d'Orsay, and I received permission from a "minister plenipotentiary" (just below rank of ambassador) to do my research there. Then toward the end of the school year at the University of Paris I was unexpectedly called to Italy.

I transferred to Italy as principal of our Italian Union Training School. This represented a setback for my doctoral studies, because practically all my research material was in Paris in the archives of the French Foreign Ministry. I plunged into my new job, got married, and the dissertation found itself for a couple of years on the "injured/inactive list," to use a term from the world of American football.

From time to time I was able to go back and forth between Florence, Italy, where I was at our college, and Paris. I got a little discouraged for a year or two, because a dissertation isn't something you can work on for a half hour or an hour, leave it, and start again. All my documents were in one place, Paris.

Plus, the archives at the French foreign ministry were very restrictive when it came to the use of their documentation. These were, after all, unique documents, handwritten, and had to be safeguarded. They didn't want this diplomatic correspondence to be damaged or to disappear. The archives were open from 2:00 to 6:00 p.m. When I was able to be there during a school break or vacation, I had to wait until 2:00 p.m. And that's what I did. But it was slow going. I had 33 or 35 big, thick, handwritten volumes of ministerial and consular correspondence to go through! It took a long time.

Finally, thank God, I received "special permission" to consult the documents in the morning as well. A bailiff would bring, just for me, the one or two bound, handwritten volumes I needed that day to a special room where I could consult them in "splendid isolation."

In due course I got back into the dissertation and took up the demanding task with renewed energy. I was pushed to do so partly because a church leader in Europe, who had himself never studied at a university, made the statement, "Beverly [most of my European childhood friends called me by my second name or derivatives of it, such as Bever, Bev, and Bevu!] will never get his doctorate, because in France you have to be a learned scholar to get a doctorate."

Remembering this, I have felt a special urge to encourage a number of scholars who worked on their doctorates over the years. Should not a leader provide encouragement to those studying and facing at times daunting problems in reaching their goal, rather than making disparaging or cynical remarks? Like other students, I needed encouragement.

At the end of May 1958 I had the oral defense of my dissertation. My major professor and doctoral advisor, Professor Pierre Renouvin, had become dean of the Faculty of Lettres. In that capacity he now had the authority to appoint the three-person "jury" (examining committee) and fix the date. This was providential.

I had noticed that dissertation defenses *always* took place on Saturday. This represented a substantial problem for me. I became concerned that years of study and research might be in vain because I would not and could not take this examination on Sabbath.

Renouvin asked me what date I wanted him to fix for the defense. In early June I was to go by ship to the United States to attend the General Conference session. I suggested the last Wednesday in May. He said that was fine, providing I turned in my dissertation by May 1. I chose Wednesday because that was the farthest away from Saturday, in case an adjustment had to be made of a day or two! I took my dissertation to Paris on May 2 to deliver four copies (two for the university library and the French National Library). How relieved I was. God must have approved of Renouvin becoming dean!

On the morning of the defense, only three weeks after I had turned in my dissertation, I had to sign in at the faculty office at the Sorbonne. The employee said, "Oh, you're the one having the lightning defense!" It usually took two or three months of waiting.

The defense lasted about two and a half hours. At the end Renouvin stood and said that the jury would now retire to "deliberate." After a half hour, which I assume included their coffee break, the jury returned, and Renouvin announced very formally that in view of the authority vested in them as dean and professors of the University of Paris, and in harmony with several relevant articles in French law, they now proclaimed me "worthy of the title doctor of the University of Paris magna cum laude." I was both surprised and elated. I had secretly hoped to get "cum laude."

A Friend Indeed

Andre Dufau, who was Jean Nussbaum's assistant, and with whom I worked in religious liberty, had a doctor's degree in law, and understood what was involved in studying at France's premier university, the University of Paris. He stood for two hours outside the oral defense room, waiting to be the first to congratulate me for successfully defending my dissertation. Then he and I went out to have lunch at a local restaurant in the Latin Quarter of Paris. I owe Dufau a debt of gratitude for being, outside of my immediate family, the most supportive person regarding my doctoral dissertation.

Then I sent a telegram to my parents in Washington with the news, and took the train to Brussels to give Eliane and her parents the good tidings. Eliane had worked very hard to type the first draft and help with the editing of the dissertation. I remember Eliane being so exhausted and almost passing out on the way to the central post office after midnight to send by registered mail some research documents to Paris in sufficient time to meet the deadline for the coming defense. We were both tired and wornout after working day and night to finish the dissertation.

With thankfulness to God, I relaxed in my seat and fell asleep on the train to Brussels.

Chapter 7

DR. JEAN NUSSBAUM

I was called to Paris as part of the team of Dr. Jean Nussbaum, who was the religious liberty man for the Southern European Division.

I went to Paris with the understanding that I was to be half-time with Nussbaum's team and half-time studying for my doctorate at the University of Paris. I had been prepared in California, with some church financial support, to go back and serve in Europe. Altogether I worked 28 years in Europe, so I think the European church got its money's worth!

Nussbaum, a medical doctor, was an interesting person. He had a great gift in knowing how to meet top people. He had married a woman who belonged to the nobility in Serbia, part of the royal entourage in some way. So Nussbaum knew that type of people. He was a charming person. He would give lectures, and, besides being a doctor, have an evangelistic campaign every year in Paris. Many people came to his meetings year after year. Some never got baptized, but they were enthusiastic supporters and liked what he said. He talked about health as well as the prophecies of Daniel and the Revelation. I was part of his team.

Nussbaum was quite a storyteller. He'd tell about his meeting with the pope, or say something like "I was meeting with Mrs. Roosevelt last week." In fact, he once introduced me to Eleanor Roosevelt. I got interested in religious liberty through him. He spoke beautiful French and had a gift of knowing how to say the right thing, both socially and professionally.

I remember on one occasion he had a personal meeting with the president of France. His evangelistic lecture was supposed to begin at 5:00 p.m. I can't prove he did it intentionally, but he arrived late for the meeting. His appointment with the president had started at 2:00 or 3:00, but at 5:00 he still wasn't around. When he showed up about 5:15, he started his lecture by saying, "Mesdams, mesdemoiselles, messieurs [he always started that way], I'm very sorry to be delayed and not be here on time, but I've just come from an important discussion in the Elysée Palace with the president of the republic." He may have arrived a little late to have an excuse to say this!

Chapter 8

ITALY CALLS

In 1952, while I was studying for my doctorate in Paris and serving on Jean Nussbaum's evangelistic team, I received a phone call telling me that the Italian Union was inviting me to serve as principal of the Italian Union Training School in Florence, Italy, the Istituto Avventista di Cultura Biblica, a boarding secondary school that featured two years of college-level ministerial training.

I had never given any thought to serving in Italy. I didn't know Italian; I had never been to Italy. And I was young, maybe too young, 24 years old. Some faculty members were almost twice my age. Why was I chosen?

My father called and said, "The education director of the division has just been to the school in Italy, and they're having a problem. The union committee can't agree about whom to ask to be principal of the school. They have two leading candidates, and each one has a group supporting him; the others are dead set against him. They don't know what to do."

Apparently the education director of the division, Otto Schubert, told the folk in Florence, "We have a young man in Paris, he's been principal of a school in California, and he's working on his doctorate in Paris. He might fit the bill here. He's already had some leadership experience in education." He said I was "intelligent." "Coincidentally," he said, "he happens to be the son of the division president."

Whether this played any role in their minds or not, I don't know. Maybe they thought the division might be sympathetic in supporting the school. But going there was not my father's plan. It was totally unexpected. It came completely from Schubert. It certainly wasn't *my* idea!

The expression "dark horse" means nothing in Italian, but I guess the folk in Italy felt I could serve as an honest broker and be neutral and objective in the internal politics of the church in Italy. I had no friends or relatives pulling me this way or that. The good of the school was my only motivation. This is, of course, as it should be.

After the call came through I asked my father for his counsel. "It would be something to consider," he said. "It's something new. It's an important school. It trains our workers for Italy and the Italian Union. Give it some prayerful thought." This I did.

So I accepted. If somebody had asked me the day before the call if I'd ever consider working in Italy, I would have said, "Italy? No." I didn't know Italian; I knew French. I thought I might be called to Collonges, or I might serve eventually in some union or local conference position. I didn't see myself as a local pastor in a church because I hadn't received specific training in that direction, although I think I could have done it, even with pleasure. I liked people, and I liked to preach. So after some thought, prayer, and consultation, I accepted the call.

It took me a full year to be practically fluent in Italian, and two years to speak it fluently in public. In the beginning I had to call a faculty member to translate for me when I needed to talk to a student. I was helped considerably by the fact that all faculty members spoke fluent French, and senior students spoke and understood French reasonably well. In fact, during my first year all faculty meetings were held in French.

I served as principal of the Italian Union Training School (Villa Aurora) from 1952 to 1958. The school had been in existence for some 12 years under the leadership of Giuseppe Cupertino, a gifted preacher, evangelist, and writer who was the "patriarch" of a well-known Adventist family and a key figure in getting the school established.

The school opened in 1940, after the beginning of World War II, when ministerial and other students from Italy could no longer go to Collonges in France. The school was run with the spirit of an enlarged Christian family at study. One of my tasks, I felt, was to develop the academic and scholastic atmosphere in harmony with denominational educational policy. I left in 1958 with the school on a sound financial basis.

After I arrived in 1952, it took me a year or so to see clearly that we would soon have serious enrollment problems if we didn't develop the secondary curriculum as well as the ministerial training. We were graduating about a dozen students each year, but the church in Italy couldn't absorb even half that many as ministers or church employees.

It was a real struggle to get the faculty and board to agree to prepare students for state examinations, but that's what we started to do. Eventually the school got full state recognition after I left the school.

The American Attraction

Italy has been a country of emigrants, to Switzerland, France, United States, South America, and elsewhere. In recent years it has also faced immigration, a new phenomenon. I took a special interest in a number of students who went to the United States. Most of them have been highly successful in their careers as church leaders, or in their personal professions, and this has given me much personal satisfaction. We have remained close friends over the years, including two and their wives whom I helped send as missionaries to Ethiopia: Alberto Sbacchi and Samuele Bacchiocchi, who both, unfortunately, died relatively young. Both had attained their doctorates. Several faculty members with me at the school went on to be significant leaders in the Italian Union: Silo Agnello became union president, Mario Vincentelli served as treasurer of the union, and Gianfranco Rossi as president. Later he became a world figure in religious liberty while serving in the division office in Bern, and as secretary-general of the International Association for the Defense of Religious Liberty. Michele Buonfiglio was a missionary and leading educator in Colombia and Venezuela for a number of years. Giuseppe De Meo served as a pastor and radio speaker for Italians in Canada. Graziano Marchi, Flavio Cella, and Willy Udovich were very successful in American business, corporate, or hospital worlds. Pietro Copiz had an outstanding educational career, completing his doctorate in the United States and serving as director of education of the Euro-Africa Division in Bern. He is also a gifted linguist. All of them became and remain my close friends.

Unfortunately, Samuele Bacchiocchi has passed away, after an outstanding career in education and building what could be called a "publishing empire."

The service in Italy was a period of seasoning for enlarged education service in the future. The Italians are wonderful, friendly, intelligent people. I owe them a debt of lasting gratitude. I could mention many more individuals; I remember them well, and with respectful affection.

A Dangerous, but Exciting Event

After a few months at the school I was working late one evening when the preceptor, Gianfranco Rossi, rushed into my office saying that a student had shot another student. My Italian was not so good, so I wasn't sure what he meant with the word *sparato,* and whether a student had been "shot" or "shot at." Rossi and I rushed into the darkness to find the two students involved. We went into the park, Rossi following me closely, and after a few minutes a Sicilian student named Anastasio appeared in the dark pointing a gun and muttering, "Cerco Copiz" ("I'm looking for Copiz!"). Romeo Copiz was the student who had been "shot at."

I was young—today I would be wiser and more cautious. I stepped up to him and said, "I'm giving you exactly 30 seconds to give me that gun!"; not knowing, of course, what I would do if he didn't.

Providentially, a strange thing happened while I looked at my watch. After 25 seconds he passed out and just keeled over. I picked up the gun and, with the help of some students, picked him up and took him to his room. Soon after, word reached me that the student fired upon was not hurt, but had jumped around the corner of the main building in time to miss the bullet. He had then run back inside, through the chapel, and hidden upstairs in the girl's dormitory. The issue between the two was a girlfriend. In the Sicilian culture of 60 years ago, this could have been a serious matter.

Place of Beauty and History
The school is a beautiful place. If you want to spend a vacation in Florence, you can get a room at Villa Aurora during the summer and pay a fourth to a third of what you'd pay at a hotel. And it's comfortable. If you plan ahead, you can have meals there. The school park is lovely. The main building, Villa Aurora, is a stately manor house from the fifteenth century, kind of like a castle, a mansion, a chateau.

People who wanted to study for the Adventist ministry in Italy came to this school, and their coursework depended on what studies they'd followed previously. Some had already studied at the university, so they would come and only study theology for two years or so. Then they would go to Collonges in France for two more years. That would qualify them, studywise, to go into the ministry. It was kind of like a junior college. It was a coeducational boarding school with about 75 students.

The six years I spent in Italy were some of the most significant, happy, and maturing years in my life. New vistas opened before me. I made lifelong friendships. I learned a beautiful, new language and basked in the Renaissance glory of Florence, its artists, and its surroundings.

A Wise President
When I was in charge of the Italian Union Training School in Florence, Italy, Luigi Beer was union president and school board chair. He was an Austrian, but he had lived in Italy for many years. In fact, he was president for more than 20 years.

When I was teaching denominational history, I mentioned how the church was organized and how there were elections every four (now five) years. One of the students commented that he thought the president was elected for life. It was understandable; Beer was already president before the student was born!

Beer was basically a good leader and deft at balancing things. The church in Italy, with all its wonderful members, had, like many committees, its factions. Beer was clever at what could be called governing by "divide and conquer" and staying above the fray. I learned lessons regarding the enduring strength of leadership that is not bogged down in partisan factionalism. A successful church or educational leader cannot be seen as a "party man."

Thinking About Something Else

Another lesson I learned in Italy was the importance of realizing that not infrequently when people talk about something, they are actually thinking of something else. They expect you to be intelligent and polite enough to understand this. This is especially important in certain cultures where it is considered impolite or even rude to refer directly to other peoples' problems or weaknesses. It took my straightforward—at times, even blunt—Bernese cultural background a spell to adapt. I had to learn this lesson in Italy, and even later, to avoid my natural tendency to deal with problems directly and in an outspoken way. The oblique approach often works better and more smoothly.

The *Intesa*

Gianfranco Rossi was the one who got the *intesa*, a legal agreement between the Italian state and our church, a law in which the state agreed to fully recognize the Seventh-day Adventist Church, indicating her rights, and the Seventh-day Adventist Church recognized its responsibility. Every Seventh-day Adventist in government employment is now allowed to observe the seventh-day Sabbath as a day of rest and worship; soldiers don't have to do routine service on Sabbath; and Adventist students are free from going to school on the Sabbath. This was groundbreaking at the time. Much of the credit goes to Rossi for his tireless efforts and diplomacy. Since then the influence of the agreement in Italy has been felt in Spain, Colombia, and also in Poland and other Catholic countries. Italian schools still function without Adventists being there on Sabbath! The *intesa* worked. It was both a breakout and a breakthrough. While we must acknowledge the help and support given to the causes of religious liberty and nondiscrimination on the part of several leading Italian statesmen and jurists, such as Francesco Margiotta Broglio, to God be the glory!

Chapter 9

A HALF-CENTURY LOVE STORY

While I was in Italy in 1954 I married Eliane Palange, my wife of more than 58 years. It's a story that began back in 1929. That's when my father had moved to Belgium as conference president and pastor of the French church in Brussels. They had both a French-speaking church in Brussels, and a Flemish-speaking church.

The Beach-Palange Connection
While they were in Brussels my father and mother became acquainted with my future wife's parents. My wife's mother, Blanche, was a Seventh-day Adventist, and her mother had been one of the earliest Seventh-day Adventists in Belgium, but not her father. For many years he wouldn't work on Saturday, but he had promised his mother he would be faithful to the Catholic Church. He was eventually baptized by his son-in-law, Pastor Roger Lenoir.

Pastor Lenoir, Eliane's uncle by marriage, has been an outstanding pastor in both Belgium and Switzerland. He has conducted, after his retirement, more than 500 Five-Day Plans to Stop Smoking. In fact, businesses, hospitals, and the Red Cross contact him to hold these plans. He has been honored by the Belgian government, and received from the General Conference Health Ministries Department its medal of honor.

My future father-in-law, Louis, was from an Adventist family in a sense. His mother was a Seventh-day Adventist, but she had died from typhus during World War I when he was 14 years old. His father remarried within a couple months, which upset the boy, and he told his father off. So he eventually had to leave his father's house and went to live with his mother's sister, a Seventh-day Adventist. He took an attic room in her house and started studying at the University of Brussels. He earned the degree of "commercial engineer." It's a degree they don't have anymore in Belgium. It was something like an M.B.A., and it qualified a person to work on the business side of industry.

While at this secular university, Louis became an agnostic. However, when he wanted to get married, he looked at the girls in the Seventh-day Adventist Church. He met my future mother-in-law, and they got married. They went to the Belgian Congo in the late 1920s, where he made a good living as the executive secretary of the company that was building the railroad in Katanga. The high point of their life there was when the crown prince of Belgium, the future King Leopold III, came and visited in their home.

Blanche prayed every night. Louis didn't oppose her, and did not interfere with her beliefs. Then my father arrived on the scene in Brussels in 1929, shortly after their return from the Congo. Blanche immediately invited my father over to their house. They were having a meal together, and my father had a conversation about the weather, politics, art, and history. Louis was very interested in art, history, music, Beethoven, those types of topics.

After dinner Blanche came out of the other side of the kitchen and whispered, "Talk to him about religion." My father thought this was not the time to do that, so my father didn't talk about religion. After my father left, Louis spoke to my future mother-in-law. "You know, this is a very interesting man. We must have him back. I want to talk to him more often." The visits continued, and he became a Seventh-day Adventist. My father baptized him. In fact, Louis Palange became a local elder of the church in Brussels, and for many years the leading lay person on the conference committee. One clear lesson emerges from this: use the right time, the right approach, and the right message to witness and help draw people to Christ.

This evangelistic approach was confirmed for me some 40 years later in St. Albans, across the English channel from Belgium. Grace Morris was our next-door neighbor. She was a fine Methodist, originally from Wales, but was now a St. Albanian. One day she came to our house and told us, to our sad surprise, that her husband of some 20 years had left her a note saying that he was leaving her. Eliane and I gave her our love, every support, and spiritual help. There was no religious pressure. We sometimes took her with us on trips to visit our churches or our college.

After a few years I had the joy of baptizing her as she joined the Seventh-day Adventist Church. She became a stalwart and appreciated member of the St. Albans church until she passed away in her late eighties. I always secretly hoped that her only child, Selwyn, a respected, professional accountant, would also join the church. That would have made his loving, admiring mother very happy.

So my parents knew my future wife's parents. When I was a baby,

Blanche used to hold me on her lap sometimes in church. Twenty years later I was studying in Paris and working with Dr. Nussbaum and his evangelistic team, and my father called me up and said, "Mother and I are planning to go to Brussels for the Easter holiday. The Belgian Conference has invited me to visit the churches. Would you like to come and spend Easter with us in Belgium?"

"Sure," I said, "anything to get away for a few days." So I took the train and met my parents in Brussels, stayed at the same hotel with them. Sure enough, Louis and Blanche Palange invited us to their home for a meal.

I was impressed by their lovely home, designed by a well-known architect, with antiques and art. However, I was even more impressed by their only child, Eliane, a slim, refined, and bright young woman of 19.

Seeing my attentiveness, my mother, always interested in my welfare and happiness, said, "You know, she could be the girl for you."

The Palanges said, "We'd like you to come for a visit." A couple months later I phoned them and arranged to stay with them for a couple days. Eliane showed me around Brussels, but she was also studying for examinations, so I spent some time simply watching her study. She always got all A's, which I cannot say for myself.

Blame It on Spain

The Palanges came and spent a week at the school in Florence during the summer, where I was living. And the next year, 1953, they invited me to go with them on a three-week trip to Spain. We saw all the sights, but for me the main sight was Eliane; and while basking in the architectural glories of Seville, I asked her to marry me, to which she "kindly consented," and we later got her father's approval, which was still proper etiquette in those days.

Within less than a year we were married.

At the 1995 General Conference session in Utrecht, the General Conference president, Robert Folkenberg, introduced me to the session as retiring from full-time, elected work for the church. I had to make a few extemporaneous remarks in response, including an appreciation to Eliane, who for nearly 50 years (at that time) had put up with and supported a "peripatetic" husband.

The session recording secretary apparently didn't clearly hear or understand the word "peripatetic," and put in the minutes that I said I was a "very pathetic" husband. When I mentioned this to Eliane, she pretended that she didn't see the error!

Chapter 10

ENCOURAGEMENT AND LIFE IMPRINTS

You get inspired when people expect great things from you. My parents always challenged me to do and be something because I was something, a child of God.

I met people in life who influenced my Christian being and lifted me up and forced me to live up to their expectations and examples. I remember such a pastor in San Francisco when I was a student at Pacific Union College (PUC) back in the late 1940s; I think his name was Chester Prout. Every time one or two friends and I came from PUC to visit the Halversons and attended his church, he would insist that we join him on the platform for the church service. He always introduced us as "senior ministerial students," which we were not. Each one of the group has made his mark, however!

Percy Christian, while president of PUC, also taught a class in the history of Latin America. Once he had to leave on a trip and he asked me to teach his class while he was gone. This, of course, forced me to study hard to prepare for the class. It also gave me a sense of empowerment, a quality we all need. It had some influence, no doubt, in my decision to later become a college history teacher.

My father took me with him while in Switzerland to be his interpreter for Sabbath sermons he gave in French and I translated into German. I thought I was helping him, but he was helping me.

Right after the war I went to Zurich to attend the German-Swiss Conference session. At the age of 17, I was appointed a delegate, an encouragement for a young person.

At one session, at a meeting for delegates and adults, the discussion revolved around "possible adulterous acts" of a minister. One older person indicated that I should leave the closed meeting because I was too young, but I pointed out that I was a *delegate!*

When I was a young principal of our Italian Union Training School, I remember a visit by my former high school (gymnasium) rector (principal) and Latin teacher from Bern. He publically referred to me as "my colleague." This was uplifting for a young man; it encouraged me to do my best.

A Humble, Dedicated Scientist

I mention a few others, in no particular order, who made their own helpful imprint on my life. The first is Henning Karstrom, a Finn. When I knew him, he was principal of the Adventist junior college in Finland, and later became principal of the Adventist junior college in Sweden. This man was a dedicated, humble Christian. In fact, he was a well-known researcher and was involved in a project that received the Nobel Prize. He was the leading assistant to the man who won the Nobel Prize. Karstrom was recognized as contributing greatly to that research project.

He gave up that important position, teaching in universities, well-known all over, to help start the Seventh-day Adventist school in Finland. He was a man of great spirituality, not interested in money or fame, but interested in serving the church and its Lord. I was greatly impressed.

Dedicated Ethiopian

Another friend was Negassa Aga, who was an Ethiopian—one of the first Ethiopians who got a degree. He was principal of one of our schools, I think the Akaki school outside of Addis Ababa. A humble person, he never acted important. Yet he was dedicated to the church. He could have worked in the government and held high positions in the ministry of education. I recommended him for the Medallion of Distinction, the highest honor the Education Department of the General Conference gives an educator. He was surprised and overwhelmed when he received it.

An Asset to Christian Education

Michael Moses was probably the first Adventist educator in western Africa to obtain a university degree, from the University of Sierra Leone. He was a man of stature, of judgment, of education. I still remember when he was arguing with people on the committee his eyes would begin to flash, the whites in his eyes apparent when the argument got a little heated.

He had a very good mind. He was accused by some of the expatriots of being a little suspect regarding his loyalty to the church. One reason was because he promoted the cause of the nationals, developing national education and leadership. But he was generally correct in his viewpoints. He was an asset to the church, convincing in his arguments, and very dedicated.

After the Biafran war I visited his school. Much had been destroyed. He was there. His house had been destroyed, but he was there. He became minister of education for the state of Imo, Nigeria. He was an outstanding man.

A Keen Theological Mind

Another person I admired was John McMillan. He was president of the British Union Conference. He was Irish, from Northern Ireland, a good Protestant. He had an incisive mind. He was a little bit critical of people with weak arguments. As a leader he was kind of hard on workers, making sure they did the right thing. I first met him when he was vice chair of the Newbold College board. Newbold had been the British Union Conference school, then it became the Northern European Division college.

McMillan was kind of argumentative, and I thought, *I'll never be able to get along with this guy.* But as time went by we became close friends. I found him clear, smart, and able to debate.

When we had the dialogue with the World Council of Churches, he was on our team in the theological discussions. He was a self-trained theologian without a university degree, but he knew theology, he knew his Bible. He may not have known all the latest, modern terms that theologians use, but he was effective.

He came to realize that my degree was not just from some "little college over in some western state with the cowboys," but from the Sorbonne in Paris. That must have impressed him. So we finally hit it off.

Later in life, after he retired as union conference president, he became pastor of the St. Albans Church where I was a local elder. We worked together in getting a church building by meeting with the Anglican bishop of St. Albans, who later became the archbishop of Canterbury. We finally got money from the division and got the church. We considered each other key factors in getting a church in St. Albans.

He actually died at a conference session, sitting on a committee. That was his life. He had no other life except his family, his church, and its activities.

Christian Gentleman and Scholar

Another person who left an imprint on my life is William Johnsson, former editor of *Adventist Review* and *Adventist World* magazines. He's been a great friend over the years. I consider him the prototypical Christian gentleman, able to present in theological conversations the

Seventh-day Adventist Church to others in a warm, winsome, and accurate way. He knows how to promote mutual understanding; he is very good at that. I came to respect him as an individual, not only as an editor and theologian, but as an authentic Christian.

A Scholar-Salesman

Another person in whom I took interest was Samuele Bacchiocchi. He came to the school in Italy when he was about 14 years old. I remember telling him years ago as a kid, "If you want to be internationally successful in our church, you should learn English."

I told him, "Go to Newbold and learn English, then if you want to go to Collonges and do some more work, fine." But from Newbold he went to America and got a degree from Andrews University. Then he ended up finally at the Gregorian University in Rome. That was after I had the division call him as a missionary to Ethiopia. He was the Bible teacher in the Adventist school in Kuyera, Ethiopia, for five years.

Bacchiocchi was outstanding in many ways. He established an industry at the school that gave it great financial support for several years. He was a salesman such as our church has rarely experienced. He was such a salesman that he was always selling, and some of his less "selling" colleagues may have felt a little bit envious at his commercial success. For a scholar, which he was, he probably overdid the "selling." Sam Bacchiocchi established a kind of private publishing empire, with a list of 40,000 people as "clients." So when he'd write a book, it would sell out its first edition just like that.

If he had gone through the denominational system, as many of us do, he might have been able to sell a few thousand copies. But he sold books in tens and even hundreds of thousands of copies, including his doctoral dissertation. Most doctoral dissertations probably don't have more than 500 copies; if you're very lucky, a few thousand.

I'll give you an example of his gifts. He studied at Newbold, and he had been the prize canvasser during the summer. When I came to the division office, he had been in Britain studying and was known as the best canvasser. He would earn tuition both for himself and for his sister, Maria, who was still studying in Italy, for the next year, and still have money to take to his parents.

When I was in the Northern European Division office in Edgware, A. F. Tarr was division president. He said, "Bert, I understand Sam Bacchiocchi is in the building today. Can you bring him by my office; I'd like to meet him. I've heard about him, but I've never met him."

So I brought Bacchiocchi to Tarr's office, and they talked for a little bit. At a certain point Tarr said to Bacchiocchi, "Give me a canvass; show me how you sell your books."

Bacchiocchi launched into his canvass, and at one point Tarr reached into his pocket to pull out his wallet. After he had his wallet open, it suddenly struck him that this was role-playing. The guy was really that good!

I can't help thinking, not very realistically, what would have happened to the Adventist publishing work if a Bacchiocchi had been in charge. It might have gone off the tracks, I don't know. But it would certainly have sold books and literature. Just a wild thought.

Invincible Integrity

A person I admire was E. W. Pedersen, who was a field secretary in the General Conference at one time, and also in lay activities. He also became secretary of the Northern European Division. In fact, he was one of my predecessors. After retirement he also served briefly as president of the Afro-Mideast Division.

He stands out in my mind, not so much for living to the age of 103 and having driven his car the very day he died, but as a man with intellectual vigor until the very end. You could talk to him about issues; he would call me on the phone about some issue in the General Conference he was concerned about. What stood out most of all was that he had this integrity and honesty; it was outstanding. I don't know of anybody who showed more rectitude, more sense of honor, or more moral courage. If he felt some worker was being mistreated by someone in the church, especially somebody in leadership, even up to the level of the General Conference president, he stood by that worker.

I don't think he was necessarily always right, but he was right about having the courage to fight for what he saw as justice. It made no difference whether it was going to hurt him, whether he would lose his job, or whatever—he would take on anybody.

You have to respect a person with that invincible integrity. In fact, I used to tell people somewhat jokingly, "I hope that if I ever commit some great sin in the church, E. W. Pedersen will be there to defend me." Since he's passed away I say, "Now that Emmanuel is gone, I'll just have to behave."

A Tower of Strength

Elisena Lucchicchia was a simple person, but very perceptive. She was a war widow and had little education, but was a hard worker who combined two professions in which she excelled: She was the cook at the school in Florence, Italy, and the school gardener. You don't find that combination very often. She was a superb cook. In fact, I used to say when

I was principal of the school, "If I have a good cook and a good dean of girls, the school will operate on a dime." Students are happy if the food is good; and the dean of girls keeps discipline. The preceptor, Anna Lippolis, did this with both charm and charity. As I write this, she's a few months away from turning 100. If we were to give Sister Lucchicchia a title today, we would call her director of food services, but we called her "cook" (*cuoca* in Italian).

She was also in charge of looking after the park. The school in Florence had a beautiful park, which it still has, surrounding an old mansion dating from the fifteenth century. It's been repaired, changed around, but it's still outstanding. In fact, it was expensive to keep up because it had all kinds of statues and paintings on the outside walls. She was in charge of the park, and she'd be out there with the students working. The students were all expected to work, they were paid. And she'd be out there with her shovel. In those days she was probably in her 50s. She wasn't a spring chicken by any means, but she was a dedicated person, and I've always admired her. She didn't have any degrees, but the students respected and obeyed her. She knew how to keep things in order.

Reciprocal Training

Pat Swan and Elaine Robinson were my office assistants. Both became assistant secretaries, one at the division and the other at the General Conference. Swan later became an associate secretary. So maybe I gave them some good training. However, they probably gave me more training than I ever gave them.

I can't mention all the many colleagues that have been important to me, many of whom I worked with in the division office in England, on the faculty in Italy, at Columbia Union College, and the General Conference staff, people who actually deserve to have a biography of their own. They are outstanding individuals. It's impossible to give a viewpoint on them in just one or two paragraphs. But I'm eternally grateful for many of these people with whom I've been able to interact, and also for the cross-fertilization that has resulted.

While writing these lines, I received an e-mail from my old friend Reinder Bruinsma, telling me that after several years of retirement following his presidency of the Netherlands Union he had been elected president of the Belgian Conference. We have worked together, off and on, for 50 years. He is a gifted writer and perceptive thinker. He is willing at times to navigate the church "ship" (an early Christian symbol) when it has to progress through choppy, even rocky, waters. I respect his courage and intellectual integrity, always alive with witty Dutch humor.

Infinite Possibilities

Ellen White wrote that Jesus discerned in every human being "infinite possibilities" as they are "transformed by His grace" (*Education*, p. 80). I have seen that potentiality fulfilled in many Christian revived lives.

Some outstanding people have not been mentioned by name. This is because of publishing constraints and also the separation caused by both time and space. Like the writer of the letter to the Hebrews, I must give up and ask, "What more shall I say?" (Heb. 11:32, NIV). The mists of history cover past friendships and associations, but their imprint is still there and their memory remains anchored in my *being* and is expanded by the ever present blessed hope in my *doing*. As I age, the beautiful hills of the Promised Land look better and better.

Chapter 11

SPEAKING WELL

I had the good fortune of living as a child in different countries and linguistic areas. Though both my parents were patriotic Americans, they believed that as missionaries they and their family should endeavor to fit and grow into the local situation and culture.

When my parents came to Paris in 1926, my father immediately engaged in a year of intense French language and culture study. He became so good at speaking French that people didn't notice he wasn't French. They thought, perhaps, that he came from another region in France. He spoke French with power and elegance, writing three books and many articles in French.

During World War II he became editor of the French *Life and Health* magazine. And since the division office was cut off from its French-speaking base in France, he sometimes had to write several articles in the same issue. His French *noms de plume* were Raymond Laroche and Gautier de la Rive.

I always attended local schools. I didn't go to an "American International school." I first learned French and spoke French like a Parisian when I was 8. That's how old I was the first time we went to the United States on furlough. I understood English because my parents spoke English in our home, but I answered in French. I didn't speak English, but in the U.S. none of my relatives (grandparents, uncles, aunts, and cousins) knew any French, so I had to speak English! It was a little like being thrown into the water: you quickly learn how to swim to survive!

From French to German

In 1936, after the furlough in the United States, my father was transferred to Bern, Switzerland, to serve as secretary of the division. I didn't go to a French school, but to the regular German school—without knowing a word of German. Matters were complicated because in Bern, people actually speak the Swiss-German (Bernese) dialect. It is quite different from

German, which is called in Switzerland "Hochdeutsch." However, in school the class was in German, and the pupils were forbidden to speak Swiss German in school. That was in order to help them learn German, their future written and formal language.

Switzerland has four national languages. If you go to the Swiss parliament, you are allowed to speak in French, German, Italian, or a language called Romanche, a little-spoken dialect in eastern Switzerland on the border of Italy, which has a connection with Latin. Probably no more than 50,000 people speak it. But it's an official language, recognized by the Swiss; like Welsh is in Wales.

I learned several languages because I had to. If you're a kid living in a French-speaking territory, which I was for the first eight years of my life, you must learn French. My birthplace, Gland is French-speaking. Then we went to Belgium and lived in Brussels. The language in Brussels in those days was overwhelmingly French. Today it's both Flemish and French. In fact, all the street signs are in two languages.

When I was 18, my first language was German—more specifically, Swiss German. In 1946 I went to Pacific Union College in California with my sister Jo Ray, and for a couple years we always spoke to each other in "Bernese," probably to the incomprehension and frustration of those around us!

Gradually English became my dominant language. But in 1951 I was called back to Europe: first to France, where I spoke French; then to Italy, where I had to learn a new language, Italian.

Many Languages—A Passe-partout to People

Plunging into new languages, even when you're young, is a challenge. But I'm grateful for the challenges that have greatly enriched my life and helped provide me with a cosmopolitan outlook. In fact, I've come to understand that it's very difficult, maybe impossible, to fully understand a people if you don't understand and speak their language. In some ways language is both the message and messenger.

At one of the General Conference sessions in the 1950s I served as translator for the evening report of the Southern European Division. We had union conference presidents from various countries speaking. Actually, I translated only from French, German, and Italian, but some came from other language areas. Many session participants probably thought I was translating from Portuguese, Serbian, Czech, Hungarian, etc. Actually, those leaders spoke German, French, or Italian. I received at the time a totally undeserved reputation as a linguistic genius.

It has been said that I am one of the denomination's linguists. I would not claim to be particularly gifted in languages, although I speak five languages fluently. But that is more a result of circumstances than of a special gift.

Today English is my primary language. For more than 50 years now I have lived in English-speaking countries (England and the United States). But when I was 8 years old French was my first language, and after that, until the age of about 20, German and Swiss German were my best languages. From 1952 to 1958 Italian became my most used language. I can still preach in these languages when the occasion presents itself.

This knowledge of languages has become extremely handy, not only inside of the church, but at meetings outside the church, such as at the Second Vatican Council, the United Nations, the World Council of Churches, the International Religious Liberty Association, Rotary International, the International Commission for the Prevention of Alcoholism and Drug Dependency, and the Conference of Secretaries of Christian World Communions. When you speak their language, people open up in a special way, particularly in a foreign country where they feel alone as strangers. I've made quite a number of close friends for this reason.

A Friend for Life

At a meeting of the Silver Spring, Maryland, Rotary Club some 30 years ago, one of the members brought a relative from Switzerland to the meeting and he was asked to speak about his club in Muri, near Bern. But the good man knew only a little English and was struggling to express himself.

After a few minutes I leaned over and said to him in Bernese, the dialect of the Swiss capital, "Why don't you speak in Bernese and I'll translate for you." I made a friend for life! In fact, after all these years we're best of friends. I've stayed in Walter Wettstein's home several times, a beautiful home with a splendid view of the Alps. He and his lovely wife, who recently passed away, are wonderful people. Unfortunately, age has caught up with him, and he is now well past 97. He had to move into a retirement facility, but we are still in friendly contact. In fact, his daughter, Suzanne, is married to a noted architect living in Alexandria, Virginia.

Linguistic Change of Personality

Another outstanding friend is Professor Jacques Robert, honorary president of the University of Paris and former justice of France's Constitutional Council. He has limited use of English; but what a vibrant personality he reveals when he speaks or writes in French! It is almost a metamorphosis. His wife, Marie-Caroline, speaks fluent English.

A few years ago I met Pope Benedict XVI at a meeting of Christian World Communions. I spoke to him in German, his native language. A broad smile crossed his face when I told him I had just come from teaching two weeks in Germany, during the German "golden autumn." Speaking to a person in their native tongue in a foreign country is almost always a warming experience.

My knowledge of French was useful when John Graz succeeded me as director of the Public Affairs and Religious Liberty Department at the General Conference. Graz had never before lived or studied in an English-speaking country. It was useful to be able to speak together in French and help Graz with his English talks and writings until he became, in due course, proficient on his own. Our secretaries probably thought we were talking about them when we spoke French together!

PART II:
DOING

"When His laborers do the very best they can, God does for them that which they cannot do themselves."
—ELLEN G. WHITE, *TESTIMONIES FOR THE CHURCH*, VOL. 5, P. 400

"I can do all things through Christ which strengtheneth me" (Phil. 4:13).

Chapter 12

INTO DIVISION ADMINISTRATION

After six years serving the school in Italy, I came to the United States and served two years at Columbia Union College, ending up as chair of the History Department.

From there I was called to be education director of the Northern European Division. That was exceptional in a way: I didn't have that much field experience for that level. That was apparently what E. E. Cossentine, General Conference director of education, thought. He held my call up at the General Conference.

A. F. Tarr, the division president, knew me; I was a friend of his son's. His son and I had gone to college together. Tarr saw me as someone who could do the job, who had intellectual capacities that the European mind would grasp and appreciate; yet who had an American background, more activist in a sense. The Europeans are more "What did we do last year, 10 years ago, 50 years ago?" They weren't willing to change easily. Tarr got the division committee to vote a call for me at the General Conference. I heard about it indirectly.

I had been teaching at Columbia Union College, but I hadn't been in touch with Cossentine much. So one day I decided to go see what he had in mind. We didn't mention any possible call—we just talked about education and our vision of the work.

About a month later the division sent the call again. The GC immediately voted it and passed it on to me. In those days the departmental men in the divisions, like the associates now in the General Conference, were elected at the General Conference session, or between sessions by the GC Committee. This was between sessions, so it was a GC Committee appointment.

The division, of course, had to decide it wanted a person. And even if the division wanted it, the GC had the final word. The GC could look at a call and say, "Have you thought about this? Is there anybody else you've thought about?"

Later Cossentine and I became good friends and colleagues. I made some excellent trips with him. He was very interested in the Seventh-day Adventist aspect of Christian education. He was strong regarding school plant and finance, but perhaps less focused on the academic side. He had the remarkable gift of arriving on campus for a school inspection and within a couple of hours he had assessed the situation! He was usually right on; but on rare occasions he could have benefited from taking more time before arriving at a conclusion. I came to respect and admire his unusual gifts and learned a lot from him.

Before a General Conference session he announced his retirement and shipped his furniture and belongings to California. Then the session insisted he stay on, and reelected him! So he "camped out" in Takoma Park for another four years. It's quite a tribute to a dedicated servant of the church.

At the 1962 General Conference session I was reelected education director of the Northern European Division, which at that time included West Africa and Ethiopia. I served for 15 years as the education director and for some six years also as Sabbath school director. Until 1975 I still had the education department. My philosophy was *Let's educate our members both academically and spiritually, both in regular schools and Sabbath schools.*

During this period we had some excellent division-wide educational conventions for the teachers, something new. This was a period in which we were able to get government recognition for our schools as gymnasiums or junior colleges. In Scandinavia, increasingly, government grants were made available to our schools, helping to develop their physical plants and augmenting teachers' salaries. The issue of government control of the schools had to be watched in order to make sure that the schools were run as Adventist schools. This we insisted on.

An amusing experience took place in Finland at our Toivonlinna secondary school and junior college. A 14-year-old student was suspended from school for a month for smoking on the public bus between school and his home. He appealed to the Ministry of Education in Helsinki, even though his parents (the father was actually a teacher at the school) fully approved of the school's discipline.

Eventually the education ministry handed down its decision, saying the school did not have the right to suspend the child for what he did off school grounds, and ordered that he be reinstated. However, the government's decision wasn't handed down until right after the suspension was already completed!

We worked on strengthening the influence of the education department. Division policy provided that the education director was ex officio member of the college and secondary school boards. Some of the union conference presidents objected to this and decided they were going to change it. They didn't inform me about it, but one of the union presidents told me about the "secret" plan.

So I came to the division winter council prepared with a battery of arguments. The only argument they had was that GC policy stated that GC and union conference officers were not ex officio members of the executive committees of the lower bodies. It wasn't difficult to point out that the division education director was not an officer and, furthermore, the school boards were not executive committees, but rather technical bodies with a different and professional task, and with much less church "political" focus.

We had quite an argument, and the matter was dropped and never resurrected again. In the end the division president, Duncan Eva, came down on my side, which I appreciated. The authority and influence of the division education department was not compromised, but grew in status and respect.

While in charge of the education department in the Northern European Division (later called the Northern Europe-West Africa Division) I helped the Adventist schools in Northern Europe get recognition as junior colleges, and government accreditation to prepare students for the European university entrance exams. Again, there was opposition from various quarters, especially from the prophets of doom, who said that the schools would never be able to get qualified teachers and meet the high government standards. But I worked to overcome these obstacles, and our schools met the challenge.

I endeavored to help school boards and faculties navigate through the Scylla and Charybdis of government grants to the schools in Europe and West Africa. I strongly pushed for postsecondary education, college- and university-level education in West Africa, particularly at the Adventist College (and later seminary) of West Africa, now Babcock University. I also pushed for the indigenization of staffs and leadership in our schools in West Africa, despite some resistance from those who felt the time had not yet quite come. I felt the time had not only come, but was overdue!

Another contribution I made to education, along with Walter Scragg, was of a different nature: in-service training for future leaders of the church in Africa. When it was planned in the late seventies to have separate divisions in Africa, I realized that it would be well if some of the most promising young workers could get in-service training on the division level in preparation for the new divisions. I'm proud that one of these promising young men came to the division office in St. Albans and served under me as assistant secretary for a period of time. He attended the officers' meetings. He must have learned well: Matthew Bediako later served effectively for 10 years as secretary of the General Conference!

After 10 years I handed off Sabbath school to someone else. Education was my highest priority. I liked doing Sabbath school whenever I had sufficient time. I enjoyed it, but education was my highest priority.

I began to "dabble" with interchurch relations as kind of a "hobby"; and that paralleled my growing career in public affairs and religious liberty.

I was also interested in secretariat work. When the division secretary was away on a trip, I usually recorded the committee minutes. There was no assistant secretary; I served as assistant secretary, not by name but in practice.

When Duncan Eva was president of the division, he used to ask me to take minutes when the secretary, Alf Lohne, was out of the office. Eva had been a division secretary for a number of years in Africa and an associate secretary at the General Conference. I learned from him how to take minutes. Eva knew how to record minutes and had the gift of wording things properly.

I remember a time the secretary of the division was away and I wrote the minutes. I gave them to Lohne after he returned and asked, "As secretary, do you want to look at the minutes? Then I'll let Eva have a look at them."

"They're fine with me," he later said. "But Eva will change everything you've written." He was used to Eva revising or touching up his minutes. Of course, Lohne's native language was Norwegian, not English. But he was fluent in English and wrote a couple books in excellent Norwegian.

So I went to Eva, and he looked over my minutes and said, "These are fine. Some of the things you've written aren't exactly as I would've written it, but it's all right that way also." He didn't change a thing.

So I went back to Lohne with the minutes and he said, "Did he change a lot?"

"He was kind of busy," I said. I didn't want him to feel that I might think I was a better recorder than he was.

During the Annual Council in 1973 Eva was called to the General Conference as a general vice president. I happened to be there with Roland Unnersten, the treasurer, and others. We had a division caucus to recommend to the GC Committee who to put in as president. The treasurer presided at the caucus because he was the ranking officer. Lohne, for some reason, was still in England. So we suggested that he come over immediately. Before Lohne showed up we agreed that he should be president. And Unnersten and the caucus suggested that I be secretary. I also kept education for two more years.

Being a division secretary is a very demanding job. There are calls being sent all the time; have the medicals been done, have the appointees been cleared? As secretary I was responsible for finding missionaries for West Africa. We were still sending out a lot of missionaries.

I didn't have much time for religious liberty, but I took an interest in Eastern Europe. In fact, that's where the liberty rubber met the road. In England, Scandinavia, and the Netherlands we had liberty. We had our schools, we had our churches. Our members were mostly able to find jobs, especially in Scandinavia if they went into fishing and had their own businesses. Of course, if you worked for somebody else you always had the problem of Sabbath observance. Labor unions were not a big issue in Scandinavia because almost everybody belonged to a labor union. To some extent they seemed almost like an arm of the government. The government did not do anything without labor unions and management agreeing. They negotiated back and forth. Once in a while they had strikes, but it's a different mentality there than is sometimes the case in the United States.

While I was in the division I took a special interest in Eastern Europe; and that was mostly Poland as far as our division was concerned. That was the only Communist country we had in our territory. I took an interest in Czechoslovakia also, because at a certain point it had a lot of trouble being in contact with the division office in Bern. The government wouldn't let anyone from the Bern office enter Czechoslovakia. So I sometimes went to Prague and met with our leaders there to talk about things and give them advice, because as far as the government was concerned, I was just a tourist from England.

Poland was different. In Poland I was on the government's list; the government knew who I was and was presumably watching me. But I was always treated very well.

I also took special interest in Hungary, and had some interesting contacts there with the Council of Free Churches and officials of other churches.

A Sad Experience

In 1979/1980 one of the last administrative tasks I had to undertake as secretary of Northern Europe-West Africa Division (NEWAD) was dealing with a serious problem in one of the division countries. Someone had made threatening phone calls to one of the church members incognito.

The telephone company was able to trace the calls to the conference office. I received calls from the conference office asking for advice. Calls had been made at times when only the president or an office secretary was there, and at least a couple of calls were made when the office secretary was outside the country. When asked, the president said, "I don't understand."

I advised the conference secretary and treasurer, "Tell him to call the police to investigate. If he's involved, he won't want to do so!"

He came a few weeks later to St. Albans for winter meetings and asked to speak to me. "I've been a fool," he said. He admitted to making the calls himself. I traveled to the city where he was located and worked out an arrangement with the conference executive committee for his resignation and a study leave. Not a word leaked out from this committee. This revealed the wisdom and integrity of these committee members, and the remarkable confidentiality and care for the church and the leader's reputation.

What had happened, it would appear, is that some lay members had strongly opposed the president's reelection at the previous session. This worked on his mind and caused unbalanced thinking. Actually, the symptoms of Parkinson's were already hard at work, and this explains how a truly "dedicated man," with a great reputation for spirituality and integrity, could do this. He passed away many years ago, respected by the Adventist Church in Northern Europe.

I stayed in the Northern Europe-West Africa Division until I came to the General Conference in 1980. I came to the GC session in Dallas as secretary of the division. But apparently some people in the division and General Conference leadership felt that after 20 years in St. Albans, and since the GC wanted me to be director of the Public Affairs and Religious Liberty Department for the world church, it was time for me to move on.

I wasn't personally excited or particularly desirous to leave and join the GC staff. I would have been happy to stay on in England as secretary of the division. I knew my job there; I enjoyed it. I was familiar with the division territories and had made many friends.

But looking back, I realize they were right. The time had come to change and meet new challenges. The fire of inspiration was soon kindled. The 25 years I spent working at the General Conference were happy and satisfying years of exciting opportunity.

Chapter 13

AN OBSERVER TO VATICAN II

In 1962 I received a letter from the editor of the *Adventist Review*, Francis D. Nichol, inviting me to go to Rome to represent the Seventh-day Adventist general church paper at the Second Vatican Council, which was to begin in September. Traditionally editors of the *Review* have been leading personalities in the church. Nichol was one such figure. You did not turn him down lightly! So I accepted the assignment, a little like Abraham, not knowing in what direction I was going.

I remember coming to Nichol's office one day in the old Review and Herald building next to the General Conference in Takoma Park, Maryland. He was a little perturbed. He said, "Bert, these vice presidents! One gives me an article, and I have to completely rewrite it. Some good sister sends him a letter telling how much she liked the article, and then he sends me another manuscript!" He threw his hands in the air. What a personality!

If I'd known the Vatican Council would last for four years, that I would be writing some 30 articles for the *Review*, I would probably have said no. After all, I had a division education department to run.

But as a result, Nichol and I became friends. And I have had the pleasure of similar friendship and collaboration with his three successors. In fact, I had the honor of serving as an honorary pallbearer at Nichol's funeral.

Why was I asked to go to Rome for the *Review*? An old friend, future editor Kenneth Wood, then associate editor, had recommended my name to Nichol, with whom I was already acquainted. To that point I hadn't done much writing, but I had lived in Italy and knew Italian. Many think the language of the Vatican is Latin, but it is actually largely Italian! Some important documents are translated into Latin.

A couple of days before the opening of the council I headed from London to Rome, but stopped for one day in Geneva to visit the World Council of Churches (WCC), hoping to get their perspective on the council in Rome, the first such Roman Catholic gathering in almost 100 years.

I tried to build wider church contacts, for the first time, in two directions: Rome and Geneva.

I had never visited the offices of the WCC and I knew nobody there, although several hundred people worked at the WCC. I knew the general secretary was Willem Visser't Hooft, but I had never met him. However, my friend John Weidner had worked with him during World War II, and Weidner told me, "When you get to Geneva, just call and tell him you're a friend of mine." This is the John Weidner of *Flee the Captor* fame. He and I had been close friends since my childhood. I became the founding board chair of the John Henry Weidner Foundation for Cultivation of the Altruistic Spirit. I have since resigned from the board, but look forward to soon seeing a new and fully researched book (and later a film, I hope) featuring the heroic work of Weidner and his Dutch-Paris Line. His widow, Naomi, is a close friend of my sister Colette's, who introduced John to Naomi!

After arriving in Geneva, I phoned Visser't Hooft from the hotel and asked if I could see him the next day. "You say you are a friend of John Weidner's?" he asked. "I'll be happy to see you tomorrow morning; just drop by my office."

That was the beginning of a knowledgeable relationship with the ecumenical movement that has lasted more than a half century. The next morning Visser't Hooft introduced me to one of the two associate general secretaries, Paul Verghese, from India, who later became Metropolitan Mar Gregorios, with whom I had various contacts, including at the Christian Peace Conference in Prague. To build bridges, one person leads to another, like a small, rolling snowball becomes a snow boulder.

Visser't Hooft told me that the WCC observer in Rome was Lukas Vischer, head of Faith and Order at the WCC, and that I should contact him after I arrived in Rome. This I did the very next day, and a friendship developed that lasted until his death in 2010. In fact, Vischer told me that he and a number of Protestant observers at the Vatican Council were staying at a certain *pensione* run by German Lutheran deaconesses, and in due course I moved there, both saving money for the church and making good contacts at morning breakfasts.

While at Vatican II I had the opportunity of meeting with some top Protestant theologians, such as Edmund Schlink of Heidelberg and George Lindbeck of Yale. Everyone treated me kindly and with respect, though back in the 1960s I was young and quite unknown.

I remember speaking in Rome with Oscar Cullmann, the well-known Protestant New Testament scholar. He told me about a suggestion he had: once a year an ecumenical offering should be taken up in all Protestant churches for a Catholic project and vice versa. I then told him about the Thirteenth Sabbath Offerings in the Seventh-day Adventist Church that benefit some project (or projects) in one part of the world. He seemed surprised and interested. Our Sabbath school offerings have indeed been a great unifying tool.

Of course, I met with some Catholic theologians and leaders, such as Cardinal Johannes Willebrands, the president of the Vatican Secretariat for Promoting Christian Unity, who felt Adventists were too eschatologically oriented; and Gustave Weigel of St. Mary's Seminary in Maryland, who emphasized that the Catholic church wanted "more unity" than Protestants, who would be satisfied with less than "organic unity" with just one church.

Hans Küng, the Swiss theologian, had breakfast with us one morning. He had a brilliant theological mind. He was a leading theological figure at Vatican II, but later had a falling-out with the Vatican. He is exactly my age, and we spoke the German-Swiss dialect together. At Vatican II he was of the opinion that Catholic dogma never had to be changed, but only renewed or developed, so that what is implicit becomes explicit. His views have evolved since then.

I had a pleasant conversation with Yves Congar, the famous French theologian and expert at the council. He had expressed some ecumenical views that were avant-garde (for a Catholic) and had problems with the Holy Office, but by the time of Vatican II he was getting in favor with the Catholic establishment. As we talked in St. Peter's in a bar/coffee shop set up for "Council Fathers" for breaks, a couple cardinals walked past and he said in French, "The cardinalate is a patent of longevity!" As a surprising sequel Congar himself, 30 years after the Vatican Council and a few months before his death in 1995, was made a cardinal by Pope John Paul II, something relatively rare for someone who is not a bishop.

Cardinal Jerome Hamer was a friend after Vatican II. He had been previously secretary of the Secretariat for Promoting Christian Unity. He had some problems with arthritis, and I arranged for him to stay for a couple of weeks at Skodsborg Sanitarium near Copenhagen in Denmark, at that time the flagship Adventist medical institution in Europe. He greatly appreciated this gesture.

One day I had lunch with Hamer and Gianfranco Rossi in Rome, and I asked Hamer point blank: "In the past the Catholic Church was opposed to religious liberty for non-Catholics, and there was the Inquisition and so forth. Now, at Vatican II, the Catholic Church has accepted religious liberty for everyone. Is it possible that in the future the Catholic Church could return to its previous position regarding persecution?"

He answered emphatically: "The change is irreversible."

Of course, he's now no longer alive. The situation could change radically with a totally new human rights climate developing. (Think of the changes caused by just one terrorist event, such as that of September 11, 2001.) Nevertheless, this was Hamer's opinion, who at that time was secretary of the "Congregation for the Doctrine of the Faith." Prior to 1960 this was the "Holy Office," and before 1904 the "Holy Inquisition."

I received press credentials from the Vatican, though I was there as an observer for our church. Technically, I was a journalist, which meant I couldn't get inside the Vatican Council *aula* (meeting hall) itself, but could attend press conferences each day and meet many bishops and other participants. Later I was allowed inside the council aula as an unofficial observer for some of the debates.

When I first arrived, I knew no one in the Vatican. I took my courage in hand and walked into the office of the Vatican Secretariat for Promoting Christian Unity (today it has been upgraded from secretariat to a council) and told them who I was. I was kindly received by an American priest, Thomas Stransky, who took me out for lunch and has been a friend ever since. He later became the head of the order of the Paulist Fathers, and finally director of the Tantur Ecumenical Center in Jerusalem. He visited the General Conference in the 1980s.

Recently Stransky moved to Washington, D.C., to stay at St. Paul's College. I hadn't seen him in a dozen or more years. Physically, he is not doing very well, but his mind is sharp and his memory remarkable. It was a joy to take him out for lunch at the Cosmos Club and "repay" him for the lunch in Rome of 50 years ago, and bring each other up-to-date regarding events and our many mutual acquaintances.

Arthur Maxwell, of "Uncle Arthur" fame and editor of *Signs of the Times*, joined me in Rome during the last session of Vatican II in late 1965. He was a man of great personality, and I always enjoyed being with him (such as at the Uppsala Assembly of the WCC in 1968).

One afternoon we both attended the press conference of American bishops. This was right after the council had voted to accept the concept of religious liberty. Maxwell, with his sense of the dramatic, asked the question: "Why did it take the 'one,' 'apostolic,' 'catholic,' 'infallible' church so long, after Protestant churches and societies accepted religious liberty years ago, to endorse and accept religious liberty?"

There was a burst of laughter in the room! Indeed, the key problem for the Catholic Church in approving religious liberty was past Catholic teaching, advocating, in effect, the persecution of those who didn't conform to its beliefs.

I met a Spanish bishop at the opening of Vatican II in September 1962. I spoke to him in Italian and said that during the past year or so we had heard a great deal about the "separated brethren," as they referred to Protestants, rather than talking about "heretics," as was the standard practice in the past. Knowing that there was considerable persecution of Adventists and other Protestants in Spain, which I knew from personal experience, I asked, "What is the relationship in Spain between the Catholic Church and the separated brethren?"

His answer was astonishing but revealing: "In Spain we have a very good situation; there are no separated brethren."

I remembered the many problems we had as Protestants: How many of our members could not get married without going to Mass, and being married by a Catholic priest if they had been baptized as a baby. How when I preached in our church we had to keep the windows shut and leave the church at the close of the service medicine dropper style, one by one, and not congregate outside the church, as good Adventists are prone to do because they are a family. Thus there would be no public evidence of a meeting.

Over the years, off and on, contacts have continued with the Council for Promoting Christian Unity. They have sent observers to General Conference sessions, and I have been invited to observe various events in Rome. Both sides know where we stand theologically. We are far apart on many issues, such as the role of the Papacy, apostolic succession, the state of the dead, the veneration of Mary and the saints. But there are also matters on which we find various degrees of agreement: the Trinity, salvation in Christ, religious liberty, service to the poor, hospitals for the sick, and the importance of marriage and the family.

Chapter 14

EARLY TRAVELS FOR THE CHURCH

First Visit to Russia in 1963

I went by train from Finland to St. Petersburg (then Leningrad), on to Moscow, and then to Warsaw, Poland. I traveled with Richard Hammill, then associate director of education in the General Conference, before he became president of Andrews University. It was a great cultural experience to see those two cities.

I was young and not as hesitant as I should have been. I didn't like seeing a picture of Lenin in every store, office, everywhere, so I asked the guide if this was one of the generals of the last war. I also sent my parents a postcard saying, "Greetings from behind you know what!"

My father didn't think that was very bright; and, of course, he was right! The outstanding experience was visiting the only Adventist church in Moscow (now we have many), which met in the Baptist church. We sat quietly in the back, trying to be as unobtrusive as possible. W. A. Scharffenberg from the General Conference Temperance Department walked in and strode with a determined step right down the aisle and sat in the front row! He was representing the International Commission for the Prevention of Alcoholism and attending an official government conference, so he wasn't a tourist, but, of all things, a guest of the Communist government!

After the service Hammill and I went with some church leaders and sat in front seats of the sanctuary, out in the open, not in a closed room, for obvious reasons. We discussed church work. I was especially touched when a sister asked: "What is the situation of our church in Spain?"

Restrictions, no church organization, problems, and all kinds of difficulties in Russia, yet they weren't just thinking of themselves. They were thinking of others, especially those being persecuted! No one could visit us at our hotel. They were not supposed to talk privately to foreigners without approval. We did meet a couple of people in a public park. How things have changed!

The WCC Uppsala Assembly 1968

We had four Seventh-day Adventist observers to the WCC assembly in Uppsala, Sweden, in 1968, including E. Murd, lead pastor of the Estonian Conference from Tallinn, the capital. This was a way to get a church pastor from the U.S.S.R. for the first time out of the country on a trip to the West. We had interesting conversations with him.

There was an issue which, to my surprise, he found significant and on which he wanted my opinion: could they ordain as a minister a pastor who had lost one finger? The issue was the Old Testament scripture requiring that priests be without physical defect (Lev. 21:17-21). In view of the many problems and longtime theological and administrative separation from the West, I was astonished that this seemed to be a major theological issue. I must confess, I felt this was "majoring in minors," to use one of my father's expressions. But after decades of almost complete theological isolation, it is quite understandable.

Our Adventist group (four observers and about as many journalists representing our publications) had daily meetings in the early afternoon to exchange information and views. On several occasions I had leading participants in the assembly speak to our group, including Roberto Tucci, a main speaker at the Assembly and editor of *La Civilta Cattolica*, a key Catholic publication, which in the days of Pope Pius XII was so important that the pope himself apparently read the proofs of this monthly Jesuit magazine.

In his address to the assembly, Tucci anticipated that the Roman Catholic Church (RCC) would become a full member of the WCC by the next assembly (which took place in Nairobi in 1975). But not long after Uppsala Pope Paul VI poured cold water on the idea during a visit to the WCC headquarters in Geneva by stating that the RCC would not be joining the WCC! The WCC tried to put the best face on this negative development by saying that the pope had now put the question of RCC membership on the ecumenical agenda! Decades later the RCC still has not joined, and, I believe, will not join, as the the WCC is currently organized. However, the RCC has considerable influence on what the WCC plans and does.

A rather humorous but revealing cold war church political event at the Uppsala Assembly took place during the election of members for the next Central Committee (1968-1975). The delegation of the Russian Orthodox Church was known to vote as a block under the rigid leadership of Metropolitan Nikodim of Leningrad, director of the Foreign Relations Department of the Moscow Patriarchate, with whom I had many contacts over the years. They were voting on the election of Charles Malik to the Central Committee, at one time foreign minister of Lebanon. Nikodim held up his hand to vote for Malik, but a member of the Russian delegation leaned over and told him that Malik was representing the Ecumenical Patriarchate of Constantinople, seen at times as a patriarchate in competition with Moscow, and not the Patriarchate of Antioch. Nikodim then gave the instruction that the delegation should vote against Malik, but since he had already held up his hand, his metropolitan dignity did not, it seems, allow him to lower his hand and change his vote. It was unique to watch the Russian delegation vote one way, and its leader vote another way! So much for infallibility!

I had a number of conversations with Metropolitan Nikodim. He was at times accused of being a Communist, even a KGB agent planted in the Orthodox Church. I doubt this was the case. I think he was trying to strengthen the position of the Orthodox Church and felt the best way to do this was to play political ball with the government and support its foreign and social policies.

Over the years he had several heart attacks; the pressures under which he labored were no doubt considerable. In 1978, 10 years after the Uppsala assembly, he died in Pope John Paul I's private papal library. About three weeks later John Paul I himself died after a pontificate of only about a month. Various stories have circulated about Vatican intrigues and the papal death, but I haven't yet seen a "who-done-it" crime story tying the two deaths (and perhaps the KGB) together! It would make for exciting, though implausible, reading.

The U.S.S.R. in the 1970s

Our church in the U.S.S.R. could not officially invite me to visit the country, because it did not have government recognition for that purpose. But the Baptists could invite me, because they had a government-approved foreign relations department. So with government approval I traveled everywhere with a Baptist conference president (originally a medical doctor), our provisional and future Adventist leader in Russia, Mikael Kulakov, and Stanislaw Dabrowski, president of the Polish Union Conference.

In every city I preached twice, once in the Baptist church, and once in the Adventist church. I was received with unbelievable hospitality. We visited the church in Odessa on the Black Sea. They had never received a visitor from outside the U.S.S.R. When I arrived at the airport in Odessa, now in independent Ukraine, I was welcomed by a large group of church members and received a couple dozen bouquets; enough that at the hotel I had to put them in the bathtub. The hotel employees probably thought I was a member of the politburo!

Every church we visited gave us gifts of appreciation. It was wonderful to belong to this great and hospitable Adventist family!

Chapter 15

LIFE-ALTERING EVENTS

Challenged by Changing Demographics

In the 1970s the British Union Conference was facing (with increased unease, even friction), what we might call race relations, or to use a less volatile and more benign expression, "human relations."

In the decades following World War II large immigrant populations, especially from the West Indies, came to Britain. They had much to offer church life. Within two or three decades they soon represented the majority of the membership, but did not hold many pastoral or leadership positions in the conferences or union. It naturally takes time for people to adapt to a totally different situation. The indigenous population believed it was being displaced, while the immigrant members felt they were being discriminated against.

The General Conference and division led out in the appointment of a blue-ribbon commission, of which I was asked to serve as recording secretary. We were charged with studying the matter and coming up with some analysis and, we hoped, make some helpful recommendations.

In hindsight that's precisely what happened. An important new concept emerged. Prior to this, I had been of the opinion that in selecting and appointing people to positions of office the criterion should be the best qualified person. That sounds reasonable and just, but it does tend to favor older, more experienced persons, and turns perhaps a blind eye to emerging and changed situations. Some may feel underrepresented and marginalized in either society or the church. From this commission I learned a new criterion and concept: the need for *representation*. That is a life-changing view. Fair representation helps deal with those who may feel overwhelmed and pushed aside, and those feeling unappreciated and perhaps discriminated against.

Shortly afterward, as secretary of the division, I led out in calling six ordained ministers from the West Indies. It was not long before Black ministers were elected to top positions in both the union and conferences in Britain, and the Adventist Church has grown and prospered greatly. However, the old problem of how to reach the vast "indigenous" population is still waiting for a propitious solution.

Computer Literacy

Back in the 1980s I noticed that computers, which I thought of as glorified typewriters, were gradually invading the office. New terms, such as cyberspace and Internet, were penetrating the rarefied atmosphere and sanctified offices of the General Conference. I didn't feel that these newfangled instruments were for me. They seemed good for secretaries, but I hadn't typed anything for some 40 years. I stopped typing when I was called to Europe in 1951 and lived in French-speaking and then Italian-speaking countries, where a typewriter keyboard and all the accents were different.

I was blessed with capable office staff and felt that correspondence and office equipment was their domain in both responsibility and expertise. Lynn Friday handled my work effectively, and I wasn't very interested in the computer she had received. It finally dawned on me that we had entered a new world—the world of the computer and the Internet. I decided that this was not for me. As the saying goes: "You can't teach an old dog (in my case, an old don) new tricks!"

Actually, I was probably subconsciously intimidated by the computer and "computerese."

I was sailing blissfully along when one day General Conference president Robert Folkenberg contacted me in a corridor of the office building. "Bert," he said, "please give me your e-mail address."

I didn't have the courage to tell him that I didn't have an e-mail address; I didn't even have a computer! I rushed back to my office and told Lynn Friday to order a computer for me, with the tacit understanding that she would operate it in my name.

However, after the arrival of the computer I was kind of attracted by the new gadget. Yes, men will be boys! I decided I should at least try to get acquainted with it. Gloria Mansfield gave me two or three hours of instruction, and despite my age, and with the help of excellent secretaries and others, a whole new world—the Internet—was gradually opened to me. That was a life-changing, horizon-expanding experience. For this I will always be grateful to Robert Folkenberg.

From this experience I learned another valuable lesson: After a hiatus of some 40 years I discovered that typing correctly, not just pecking away and discovering keys Christopher Columbus-style, was still in my fingers. What a discovery and life lesson: Life's habits remain with you, even when we are not aware of them. They're always there, even subconsciously.

I had assumed that I would have to learn to type all over again. I had taken two quarters of typing from Mrs. Miriam Utt at Pacific Union College in 1946/1947. I couldn't believe that after all these decades, typing was still in my mind and fingers. I could type, to some extent, without even looking at the keyboard, thanks to a good teacher.

This is also a valuable spiritual lesson: It's important to cultivate good habits. What we learn or do is indelibly registered and remains with us, though we may not consciously realize it. That's why the apostle Paul invites us to think and focus on that which is true, pure, and lovely (Phil. 4:8). Both good and bad habits leave a lasting imprint.

Chapter 16

A RELIGIOUS LIBERTY LESSON

About 1956/1957 a former student of mine at Villa Aurora, Giuliano Di Bartolo, was doing his required military service when he contacted me at the school in Florence about having a Sabbath problem. The next Sabbath they were having required exercises, and he was told he would have to attend.

I called Gianfranco Rossi in Rome, and he and I went to the military camp at Arezzo and asked to see the colonel commanding the regiment. We met with him and the company commander, a captain. We made our case in favor of religious liberty and respect for the conscience of the young soldier, but we didn't get very far.

The colonel said that the exercises included the use of hand grenades and involved teaching how to avoid certain dangers, and that it was impossible for Di Bartolo to be absent. I felt things were moving in the wrong direction.

Suddenly the captain said that it was too bad if arrangements could not be made for Di Bartolo, because he was the "best soldier" in his company. Miraculously, the colonel changed his viewpoint immediately, and he soon said, "Here in Italy, of course, we respect individual conscience and the religious practices of our soldiers. We will make arrangements for Soldier Di Bartolo!"

I had just learned my first great lesson of religious liberty work: If a person (employee, member of the military, student, etc.) is doing good work and is liked and respected, it is much easier to have success in obtaining Sabbath privileges. Our church members have to be aware of this.

It's important to be a capable, faithful, and "conscientious worker," not just a person with "conscientious beliefs."

Chapter 17

CZECHOSLOVAKIA: FROM BANNED TO FREE

Back in the fifties and sixties Czechoslovakia had serious religious liberty problems. Our church had been banned and all its properties confiscated, including the headquarters in Prague and the training school.

After a couple years the government allowed us to work out of two or three rooms on the ground floor of the large building we owned. The building was four or five stories tall and had a church sanctuary that was then being used as a rehearsal hall for a government orchestra.

The Southern European Division office in Bern was not permitted to have regular contact with the union conference office in Prague. Even though Czechoslovakia wasn't part of the Northern European Division territory, I decided to stop off in Prague on my way to Warsaw, Poland, knowing my name wouldn't be on the government's list of the division staff in Bern.

In Prague I walked to the small "remnant" of the union office. I wanted to encourage the leaders there, to let them know they weren't forgotten, and to find out what the situation was.

I met with O. Sladek, the union conference president. It was the beginning of a friendship, especially since Sladek spoke good German but, at that time, very little English. Sladek phoned Pastor Miloslav Sustek, who was a close informal advisor to Sladek, and asked him to come to our meeting.

Sustek had studied at Collonges in France and served for a short time as a pastor after World War II. But when the Communists took over the country and the iron curtain came down, Sustek could not be ordained. Instead, the government shipped him off to the coal mines and banned the church.

Sustek was eventually allowed to return to Prague and serve as a receptionist in a hotel, where even an obscurantist totalitarian government realized that his great gifts as a linguist could be put to better use. Besides

85

his own Czech, Sustek spoke excellent German, French, English, Russian, Latin, and a smattering of other languages.

After Sustek arrived, Sladek and I had a couple hours together, during which we accomplished what the French call a *tour d'horizon* of the current situation. I remember several interesting aspects of the meeting.

At a certain point Sladek got up, opened the window, and looked out briefly to make sure no one outside was listening. Before we parted with prayer, Sladek asked us to remember what we had talked about. We agreed that we had discussed the translation and production of the Sabbath school lessons, which was true (I happened to be Sabbath school director of the Northern European Division at the time), as well as some other matters. The reason for this was that if we were interrogated separately by the security police, we could each tell essentially the same thing. That was the climate in which church leaders lived in Eastern Europe in the sixties and seventies!

Moving forward a few decades: in early 2005 a meeting took place in the palatial Senate Chamber of the Czech Republic. The meeting was a religious liberty conference sponsored by both the Czech branch of the International Religious Liberty Association (IRLA) and the Adventist Development and Relief Agency (ADRA). Adventists were the main organizers of the meeting. John Graz, secretary general of the IRLA, was present, an Adventist sat in the speaker's chair, and I was the keynote speaker. I reviewed the ups and downs of more than 40 years of religious liberty in Czechoslovakia. Who would have imagined in the sixties or seventies that such a change could take place?

When you're on God's side, you're on the winning side.

Chapter 18

TRAVELS IN AFRICA

My life has usually been without significant international incidents. When you travel and represent the church, caution and prudence need to be the order of the day. For example, while visiting and traveling in Communist Poland for some two-score times, with many visits to government and church leaders, not once was there a problem. During all these years of travel to some 140 or so countries, I was "arrested" ("detained" is probably a more accurate, less loaded term) only twice, and both times when I was in Ethiopia.

The first time it was at Debre Tabor, where there was an Adventist hospital and mission station. Dr. Kristian Hogganvik was the dedicated missionary there. He took care of everything. When I arrived there the first time by plane from Addis Ababa, landing on a grass strip, I found Hogganvik underneath his old car, repairing it. He was not only a fine doctor, but a good mechanic, an excellent pioneer missionary.

I was in the little town with Dr. Houmann, one of our dedicated missionary doctors in Addis Ababa. Dr. Houmann had a movie camera, and a police lieutenant in the town stopped us, saying we were making maps! This was of course nonsense. He also claimed that my visa was outdated, which was also not true. He had looked at the date the visa was issued in London by the Ethiopian embassy, not its validity date! After some discussion at our mission station and when he heard that he was dealing with the physician of the imperial family, he decided to drop the matter. To simplify things, our mission director, Tebedge Guddaye, had told him the dates in my passport were the European calendar, not the Ethiopian one!

The second incident was in Eritrea, which was then part of Ethiopia, but there was already an independence movement that caused the authorities to be very security conscious. The Adventist mission headquarters and school were located very close to a military camp. When getting on a bus near the mission, I was stopped and ordered off the bus and taken to the military camp. An informer had said that I had been on the nearby hill taking pictures of the camp. This was pure fiction. I hadn't been on that hill and had not taken any pictures.

I finally got to see the colonel, who spoke English, and when he heard I was from the Adventist mission station and an official of the church, everything was dropped and they apologized for the error.

Another time I was stopped at the Port Harcourt airport in Nigeria as I was leaving the country. I was traveling with my old friend Charles Hirsch, education director of the General Conference. I was accused of transporting arms into the country. This was just weeks before the Biafran civil war broke out, so security personnel were on edge. The objects of their concern were a couple of decorative spearheads made for tourists that I had obtained in Ethiopia during our visit to various Adventist schools. I explained this to the officer and pointed out that, furthermore, I was not at this point bringing anything in, but taking things out! Everything was resolved amicably. I still have the spearheads somewhere in the boxes of things I collected while traveling, and they're waiting to be displayed—when my wife permits!

I remember visiting a Yoruba chief in Nigeria on one of my first trips to Africa and asking him how many children he had. All the subchiefs present laughed. That was not the appropriate question to ask! He amiably, and with indulgence, answered that he had about 30 sons, but was not so sure about the number of daughters!

I love dealing with Africans. I have always treated them as equals, neither disfavoring them nor overindulging them. They have always responded by treating me as a friend and with respect. Respect engenders respect. I love their contagious humor, optimism, and happiness.

Blessed Fulfillment in Growth

One of my great joys and satisfactions has been to see the tremendous growth of the Adventist Church, its institutions, and members, during the past 50 years. In countries such as Ghana and Nigeria, there has been a church development boom! It is wonderful and most encouraging. It is very gratifying to know I had a small part in the development of the church; creating conferences out of missions, greatly expanding postsecondary college and graduate education, and training and preparing respected and successful church leaders, ready to serve in their homeland or at division and even General Conference levels. In fact, some of these bright stars now serve the world church at all levels, including the General Conference. The sometimes tiring and uncomfortable trips are now looked back upon as wonderful and blessed missionary and spiritual "safaris."

After the Rainy Season

It may surprise some to hear that in hot, sunny equatorial western Africa considerable morning fog can interrupt plane schedules. Fifty years ago travel, even by Land Rover, could be very difficult on the other side of the continent in areas of Ethiopia. Certain parts of the country had no roads, only tracks that were largely unusable by vehicles during the rainy season. Each rainy season made some changes in the direction and use of the tracks. They resembled dry or muddy creekbeds full of holes and boulders.

I remember one trip west from Addis Ababa to Gimbie on the famous "Gimbie Road." This trip was soon after the rainy season, and took three days. Today you can do it in three hours or so, when the road is maintained. We had two vehicles, and I was driving the second, a Land Rover. We were bringing two missionary wives and children to their doctor and school principal husbands, who were already on location. We had to camp out in the open one night, and this gave me the opportunity to see a leopard flash by in the starry night.

We crossed a stream, and the first vehicle broke through the primitive bridge made of tree limbs, almost tipping over into the stream below! We were compensated for all the trouble, even danger, by witnessing the joy of the reunions of these fine missionary families, the Saunderses and the Kuhns, when the husbands came out to meet us as we approached Gimbie.

On another post-rainy season trip I traveled south from the capital to look into establishing a new mission station in the southern part of Ethiopia, where the church was rapidly growing. I was with Erik Palm and his wife, Ingrid, sterling pioneer missionaries from Sweden and worthy of the best Vikings. Once when we got stuck Erik and Ingrid, who I suppose were in their sixties, shoveled and pushed the car to get it out of the muck and upright again.

We arrived at a lovely natural location, with as yet no running water. But there was a cave nearby with a waterfall formed by a little natural spring near the entrance. The local population no doubt found it interesting, probably even amusing, to see these strange, recently arrived, white-skinned adults, showering to get rid of the grime of the trip. It was their children who "played" in the waterfall. However, a new mission station was on its way. God had protected and guided us.

In the Danakil Desert Plain

Writing these memoirs has refreshed my aging memory regarding a unique trip in Ethiopia more than 40 years ago in the hot and parched

Danakil Desert. I traveled with Solomon Wolde-Endreas and his wife. He was a young and up-and-coming minister, and she a trained nurse. Since then he has become a leader of the church in east Africa, not only in Ethiopia and Eritrea but also at the division level. It has been difficult in recent years to keep the church going in Eritrea, because of the severe lack of religious liberty.

We were traveling to reopen the recently established mission station/clinic on the Awash River in the Danakil Desert plain in northeastern Ethiopia. The station had to be shut down during the blazingly hot summer season. Traveling on the road was comparatively easy as we sailed along trying, it seemed, to keep up with the ostriches and other wildlife running ahead of us.

We were hot and tired when we arrived in the early evening at the small station on the Awash. The first thing we had to do, after thanking the Lord for a safe trip, was to get the generator going to provide light and electrical power. The water we had was lukewarm and quite unrefreshing. I was reminded of what Christ said about the Laodicean Church in Revelation 3:16: "So, because you are lukewarm—neither hot nor cold—I am about to spit you out of my mouth."

How nice it was to get up in the middle of the night, after the restarted refrigerator had enough time to cool it, and get a cool drink of water!

The Danakil people belonged to a Muslim sultanate, but also practiced many Afar indigenous religious practices and traditions. They were no doubt happy to see the nurse back, and the station open again.

The next morning we walked to the river and saw several crocodiles slip off the riverbank into the water as we approached. It surprised me to see young men with small boats navigate the river, even jump into the water despite the threat of crocodiles. I was told that on rare occasions a person got caught.

Bert as a baby in Brussels, c. 1931

Bert's parents while living in Bern

Bert and sister Jo Ray at the Belgian seaside, c. 1933

Bert, c. age 10

Bert skiing in the Bernese Alps

Bert with his tennis racket in Bern (middle teens)

Above: Freies Gymnasium athletic team (c. 1945): Hai Herzog (front row, far left) and Bert (front row, far right)

Right: Bert in his attire with sash and sword as president of the Patria Bernensis school fraternity

In Texas (1936) with Grandfather Corley (holding Colette), grandmother, and two aunts. Front right: Bert and Jo Ray.

Bert at time of "engagement" in Brussels (1953)

Eliane and Bert at Palange home on their wedding day (1954)

Bert as school principal in Florence, Italy (c. 1953)

Eliane (right) with Gianfranco Rossi and his wife, Carmela, at Barzio, Italy

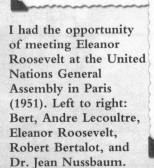

Above: Walter Beach and Bert in their doctoral robes at a Newbold College graduation.

Left: Bert

I had the opportunity of meeting Eleanor Roosevelt at the United Nations General Assembly in Paris (1951). Left to right: Bert, Andre Lecoultre, Eleanor Roosevelt, Robert Bertalot, and Dr. Jean Nussbaum.

Meeting of Secretaries of Christian World Communions in North Carolina, where Bert announced his retirement. Eliane is next to him on the front row; John Graz is in the middle of the picture.

Right: Participants in the dialog between Lutherans and Seventh-day Adventists. Bill Johnsson is in the third row, far left; Bert, front row, far right.

Bert (middle front) at fiftieth anniversary (1998) of the class of 1948 at Pacific Union College

Right: John Tarr, Bert, Eliane, and Jo Ray in California.

Meeting of United States church leaders in Asheville, North Carolina

Bert receiving the Knight's Cross of the Polish Republic

Bert (with Eliane) receives honorary membership in the Polish Bible Society from Barbara Narzinska (2001).

The Lord Chamberlain is
commanded by Her Majesty to invite

Doctor and Mrs. Bert Beach

to a Garden Party at Buckingham Palace
for those attending the Lambeth Conference
on Tuesday, 28th July, 1998 from 4 to 6 p.m.

This card does not admit

Invitation from Queen Elizabeth to a garden party at Buckingham Palace

The Archbishop of Canterbury and Mrs Carey
request the pleasure of the company of

Dr Bert Beach

at Lunch on Tuesday 28 July at 11.45 am for 12.00
at Lambeth Palace
In Honour of the Bishops of the Anglican Communion

R.S.V.P.
Canon Andrew Deuchar
Lambeth Palace
LONDON SE1 7JU

Day Dress
Please bring this
invitation with you

Invitation from Archbishop and Mrs. Carey to a lunch at Lambeth Palace (1998)

Meeting of IRLA experts in Spain. Bert (second from right) is sitting between Archbishop Roland Minnerath and Mitchell Tyner.

Bert (far left) and Gianfranco Rossi (middle right) meeting with president of Portugal (far right)

Bert (on right, next to Metropolitan Ibrahim) attends a dinner by the division for leading participants of the WCC Harare Assembly. The archbishop of Uganda (second on left) was killed by Idi Amin shortly after this picture was taken.

Bert's parents with his sisters, Jo Ray (left) and Colette

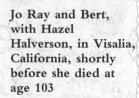

Jo Ray and Bert, with Hazel Halverson, in Visalia, California, shortly before she died at age 103

Bert, at La Sierra University graduation, gives former president Arias Sanchez of Costa Rica the first John Weidner Medal for Altruism.

Bert gives a medal to the prime minister of Burundi.

Above: Bert with the president of Iceland

Right: Bert gives the president of Albania a plaque of recognition after the fall of totalitarian Communism in that country.

Bert speaks at a General Conference dinner honoring Emmanuel Pedersen on his 100th birthday, with a smiling church president, Jan Paulsen.

Bert shakes hands with Pope John Paul II after a lunch inside the Vatican.

Bert speaks in German with a smiling Pope Benedict XVI.

Bert arranges a meeting with his friend Robert Runcie, the archbishop of Canterbury, for Ralph Thompson, Neal Wilson, and W. R. Beach (left to right)

Bert with his two daughters, Danielle (a lawyer) and Michele (an educator), and his three grandchildren. *From left to right:* Alyssa Izzo, Michele Beach-Izzo, Philippe Beach Evers, Danielle Beach, and Emma Izzo (2012).

Regular panel members of the American Religious Townhall weekly telecast.
Front row, left to right: Bishop Othal Lakey, Monsignor Michael Olson, Bert B. Beach, Dr. Carl Trovall.
Back row, left to right: Rev. Ray Flachmeier, Moderator Jerry Lutz, Rabbi Jordan Offseyer, Rev. Tom Plumbley, Dr. Mel Robeck, Canon John Peterson.

Bert and Eliane, now happily retired, on an Alaskan cruise in 2011 with the American Religious Townhall board.

Chapter 19

SPEAKING THE TRUTH

"Solidarity" was the liberating democratic movement in Communist Poland. In Warsaw I visited the central office for Solidarity with Ray Dabrowski, at the time editor for the Adventist Church in Poland, and later, for 15 years, communication director for the General Conference. He had a creative streak at a time of unventilated minds. A man approached me and asked for directions. I mumbled something that was neither Polish nor English and walked away. I didn't want to draw attention to myself, an American, at a time of tension and martial law in Poland.

Over the years I learned about dealing honestly with Communist government officials. I didn't always say everything I was thinking, but what I said was true. Usually the officials treated me with respect, even honor. They greatly resented church leaders thanking them for treating the church well, then reporting back to Washington or elsewhere that they had been behind the iron curtain and how bad the situation was!

I never thanked them for the religious liberty they gave us, but rather for positive relations and for recognition of our church; and I told them of our desire to work for the welfare of the country and its people. Sycophantic subservience is seen for what it is: a lack of sincerity.

I learned that Communist governments did not want surprises. It's generally wrong, at least in those cases I've had to deal with, to say Communist governments imposed chosen or secret Communist agents as leaders of our church. They wanted leaders whom they already knew and had seen in action. They expected leaders to move up from other positions. In other words, a union conference president was expected to have been union secretary or conference president. The same applied to other positions.

In Communist countries the concept of the General Conference (and division) being the highest spiritual and doctrinal authority in the national church was often acceptable. But they wanted nationals to run and administer the national church. Usually in Eastern Europe they were quite willing to acknowledge the spiritual authority and advisory role of the General Conference world church.

Dealing with the Communist regimes of Eastern Europe for more than 30 years was an interesting but not easy task. It took patience, diplomatic adroitness, and versatility. It also took some appropriate protocol skills to deal with heads of state, prime ministers, cabinet ministers, chief justices, governors, and heads of churches. You don't learn these skills overnight. You make some mistakes, but you learn. I discovered that top people tend to be more forgiving than their underlings. We are told that "the smaller the station, the bigger the stationmaster."

I was obviously seen as a church leader from the West. I'm sure that people in Communist countries didn't want me, once I was invited to visit their country and treated as a favored guest, to go back and publish negative, one-sided, or tendentious information about them. I didn't have to. I followed the approach of being honest with them, and did this at times with some humor and a smile on my face. I did not engage in false and hypocritical compliments, which both sides usually know is not meant!

I remember one Communist government official complaining to me about this. I thanked them for the understanding we had and for the contribution they had made to rebuild after the war and lift the economic and health standards of living. I pushed, of course, for greater freedom and recognition for the church, but always step by step. I always made it clear that the church's leaders in these countries are chosen by their own people and not by leadership abroad. We were just advisors, and I sometimes used an illustration my father had used earlier:

I said that the president of the church in, let's say, Poland or Hungary, was like the father of a family who is in charge of his children, but he at times gets help or advice from others, like the plumber or the shoemaker. "I come like the doctor or electrician at the invitation of the father," I said. The church in their country runs its own administrative affairs, finances, and elections, but recognizes that it belongs to the worldwide spiritual Seventh-day Adventist family, the General Conference, which has doctrinal and spiritual authority. I found that Communist governments, with only a few extreme exceptions, could live with this concept.

An incident that happily didn't get much notice, but was uncomfortable for me, took place during a meeting of the Christian Peace Conference in Prague. During the cold war period attendance at this conference allowed us to visit Adventist churches and leaders located in the Eastern European Communist countries.

One of the speakers at this meeting of several hundred people was a left-wing American who in his speech attacked United States foreign policy, the Vietnam War, and, at least by implication, supported the policies of the Soviet Union. The "well-trained" audience stood up and applauded. However, one person in the audience remained seated. It was uncomfortable, but I was not, especially in a foreign country, going to participate in this unbalanced propaganda attack against the very country, although imperfect, that stood for democracy and both civil and religious freedom for which these Eastern Europeans were yearning and would still have to wait for several years.

Chapter 20

PUBLIC AFFAIRS AND RELIGIOUS LIBERTY— NEW GLOBAL APPROACH

In 1980 I was appointed director of the Public Affairs and Religious Liberty Department for the Seventh-day Adventist world church, the General Conference (GC).

I very much enjoyed my work as secretary of the Northern Europe-West Africa Division (NEWAD), first with Alf Lohne as president for two years, then with Walter Scragg as president. Both were gifted men, and I enjoyed working with them. I think we complemented each other in several ways.

For more than 20 years Roland Hegstad, the creative spirit and ideologue of the department and editor of *Liberty* magazine, had been a key member of the General Conference department. Earlier he approached me indicating that he would like to see me at the helm of the Public Affairs and Religious Liberty (PARL) Department. His desire was to turn the department into a kind of Seventh-day Adventist "state department"; a worthy goal, but not fully feasible as the church is organized. The concept would cut across functions and interests in which presidential, secretariat, and some departments are involved. The idea had some merit and was used to some extent in the reorganization of the department that I was involved in.

Immediate Goals

I had several immediate goals when I came to the department: First, I wanted to make the department fully world-oriented, rather than U.S.-centered as it had largely been in the past. Second, I wanted the department to emphasize public affairs, that is, ongoing government relations rather than solving religious liberty problems piecemeal as they arose. Third, I envisioned the two liaison offices between the church and the U.S. Congress and the United Nations being included in one PARL department. Fourth, I hoped to assign the protocol functions of the General Conference to PARL, which previously had been dealt with primarily by the Communication Department. Fifth, I wanted to establish a council for interchurch/faith relations at the General Conference.

General Conference president Neal C. Wilson saw wisdom in these approaches, together with other officers, and this reorganization began taking place. I was blessed in having, for a decade, five very capable associates, each with their own mind and strong, well-articulated opinions. We didn't always agree with each other; but we respected each other, we worked together, and we remained good friends after retirement. Neal Wilson and his fellow officers were very supportive and provided perceptive advice.

Broad Church Interests

My first love was Adventist education. However, I developed other interests:

1. Church governance and denominational policy. Together with Walter Scragg, I rewrote and organized the Northern Europe-West Africa Division *Working Policy*. This also became the basic working policy for the newly established West-Central Africa Division after 1980. During the late seventies I was the "expert" of the NEWAD regarding the retirement policy and its application to nonroutine cases. I also served on two General Conference governance and church organization study groups under both Neal Wilson and Robert Folkenberg.

2. When the General Conference decided to have "rules of order," I was asked to draft them for approval by the General Conference Executive Committee. I took the view that the General Conference serves the world, and thus should not simply appoint *Robert's Rules of Order*—U.S.A. -produced and -oriented—as its procedural authority, but have its own, albeit very much influenced by *Robert's*. I wrote an introductory philosophical statement, which points to the different natures of the Seventh-day Adventist Church and political bodies. The GC rules still stand today with some minor revisions prepared together with attorneys Walter Carson and Todd McFarland.

3. Wide range of writing: spiritual/inspirational, theology, church history, religious liberty, church-state relations, social responsibility, ecumenism, Catholic Church, prevention of alcoholism and smoking, Rotary, public statements by the church, travelogs, guidance for ministers and laity.

Chapter 21

CRISIS IN NICARAGUA

Not long after I came to the General Conference, we were confronted with a major crisis in Nicaragua during the Sandinista regime. I had visited Nicaragua earlier and discovered some tension in that country between the church and the government. When I asked to meet with some government leaders, I was told by church leaders that they avoided contact with the government in order to not draw attention to the church in the hope of avoiding problems. That approach to public affairs surprised me, to say the least.

I felt this wasn't a good way to deal with the issues. If officials don't know you, they can easily develop inaccurate and negative concepts regarding the church. Unfortunately this has been the case at various times and places, and some of the fault is the church's.

One morning in 1982 at the office in Washington, D.C., I received word from George Brown, Inter-American Division president, that Nicaraguan authorities had closed our administrative office in the capital, Managua, as well as all our churches and schools throughout Nicaragua! The "lay low" policy had obviously not worked, and caused us now to "lay flat."

I asked my old family friend James Aitken, who represented the General Conference Public Affairs Department at the United Nations (U.N.), to contact the Nicaraguan ambassador at the U.N. Aitken was told we should contact the Nicaraguan ambassador in Washington, who also served as ambassador to the U.N. I contacted him and invited him to come for lunch at the General Conference in the next day or two, if at all possible.

To my surprise and great relief, the ambassador readily accepted the invitation. This was an answer to prayer. Ambassadors do not normally visit the General Conference without previous contacts over a period of time. He came the very next day. I also invited George Brown to fly up to Washington from Miami for the meeting. I acquainted the ambassador with the critical problem and told him that as a church we cooperate with all governments. I assured him we were not "involved with the CIA," which was a key accusation used by the government to close us down in Nicaragua.

After some further questions and discussion, the ambassador stood up and said, "Tomorrow I am leaving for Nicaragua, and I will be meeting with the three-man junta running the government. I will be your spokesman."

This was providential. Before hearing about our problem, he had already had plans to fly to Nicaragua.

For several days we heard nothing. Then word reached us that the government had reopened our mission office and all other church properties. The government stated to the press that its ambassador in Washington had assured them that the Seventh-day Adventist Church was loyal to the nation and not an arm of the CIA!

There's a sequel to this story: After the ambassador returned to Washington, I invited him and his wife out for dinner at the Cosmos Club. At first he said yes, but then said he could not, because on the given evening he was going to be at our Capital Memorial church in Washington, D.C., for a Daniel and Revelation Seminar.

"My wife and I will come and join you," I told him. "Afterward we can have dinner together." That's exactly what we did. God's resources are unlimited. He can send an army of angels, or just one ambassador: the right person, in the right place, at the right time.

Chapter 22

RECOGNIZED BY THE UNITED NATIONS

The United Nations is significant for its influence in society, especially in human rights and matters of international relations, war, and peace.

Religious Liberty at the United Nations
The Universal Declaration of Human Rights was voted by the U.N. in 1948, a few months after I graduated from college. While in Paris I was honored to meet Eleanor Roosevelt, who had been a forceful advocate of religious liberty. She had been president of the U.N. Human Rights Commission and involved in getting the declaration voted. Article 18 forcefully upholds religious liberty in multiple ways, including the right to change religion.

For several decades we worked to get the U.N. to vote the so-called religious liberty declaration. When it was finally voted in 1981, we were able to get included a statement upholding the right of every person to "observe days of rest . . . in accordance with the precepts of one's religion." All this took several years and many contacts with various delegations and ambassadors.

My old colleague Gianfranco Rossi was especially helpful. Religious liberty promotion often requires long, persistent, and patient efforts to legalize religious freedom. This is where he shined. This involves having ongoing contacts with political and diplomatic figures, suggesting language drafts, and pointing out violations of freedom. Thus, it is important to know people, and to be known by them. Knowing another language is a plus, and knowing several other languages is a plus plus! It is necessary to grasp past history, understand cultural and other influences, and know where people come from and in what direction your interlocutors are moving or want to go. It helps to be seen as having a wide, nonsectarian vision, and working for human dignity and nondiscrimination, and the rights of all people, not just your church members or the citizens of your country.

In public affairs it is difficult to work in isolation and achieve success; if you isolate yourself, you risk becoming suspect. I have always been encouraged and lifted up by knowing that we are both on God's side and on that of persecuted or downtrodden human beings. For me it was great to be in New York on November 25, 1981, and listen and see the religious liberty declaration voted by the U.N. General Assembly after decades of discussion, delaying tactics, and outright opposition. When you are on God's side, you are on the winning side.

After being appointed to the General Conference Department of Public Affairs and Religious Liberty (PARL), I wanted to build contacts for the church in New York and Geneva, where the two main offices of the United Nations are located. Earlier the General Conference had appointed two individuals to serve as liaison for the Adventist Church, one for the United States Congress and the other for the United Nations. After I came to the General Conference, I recommended that these positions come under the direct purview of PARL, as associate directors, and this has been the case ever since.

For a decade Gary Ross served as the first PARL congressional liaison. With his keen mind he broke new ground. James Aitken was the first part-time U.N. liaison in New York and established a number of helpful contacts. He obtained for the General Conference nongovernmental organization (NGO) status with the U.N. Public Affairs Department. This gave the church access to the U.N. building and the opportunity to receive various U.N. documents and reports, but not the right of public intervention.

I soon discovered that the more significant NGO status was to be in consultative status with the Economic and Social Council (ECOSOC) of the U.N., one of three key U.N. bodies. The other two are the Security Council and the World Court.

Achieving consultative relationship with ECOSOC was not easy. Many organizations wanted this status. A specific committee dealt with the recognition of NGOs. Many were not accepted, although outright rejection was rare. What usually happened was that the application would simply be deferred for another year or two, or more.

I remember a representative asking for the committee to give a yes or no answer. His organization's application had been deferred for about eight years. Part of the problem was that the committee worked by "consensus," and representatives from Communist countries would take turns referring the application until the next year by issuing such statements as "My government has not been able to study the application as yet" or asking "for additional information."

I noticed that several organizations were turned down because they had a presence in South Africa, where apartheid was still practiced. To help counteract this potential problem, I asked then-secretary of the General Conference, G. Ralph Thompson, to come with me to the meeting in New York. Coming from the West Indies, he made a favorable presence sitting at my side. I believe God was with us, and only insignificant questions or challenges were presented to us. We were the last NGO approved that year before the committee adjourned after 10:00 in the evening.

Another factor was helpful and providential: The secretary of the NGO committee, a career U.N. staffer named Pilar Santander Downing, was the mother of the roommate of my nephew, Walter Witt, at Yale University. She was able to keep me posted and helped to guide the matter to fruition.

Some 20 years later we were able to get the International Religious Liberty Association to receive the same NGO status. Jonathan Gallagher, then U.N. liaison and associate director for PARL, was mostly responsible for achieving this result.

We now have three different organizations we can use to represent us, the third one being the International Association for the Defense of Religious Liberty, founded by Jean Nussbaum, professionalized by P. Lanarès, and brought to increasing influence by Gianfranco Rossi and his successors, M. Verfaillie and K. Nowak. In fact, I was able to help them get this association upgraded from "on the roster" to Category II NGO, the same status the other two bodies have.

This status gives us the right to both speak and send written interventions at meetings of the Human Rights Commission in Geneva. It is a right we have used regularly, albeit with discretion. A change at the U.N. has now replaced the former Human Rights Commission with the Human Rights Council. It is harder to get the opportunity to speak, but written interventions still function. We don't want to create problems in certain countries by arousing government or media hostility. We want to solve problems with "quiet diplomacy." Many difficulties can be better dealt with by respectful, soft-hued, unexcited discussion and mediation, rather than bringing in the "cavalry" or using a "gunboat" approach.

Of course, sometimes a strong hand is necessary. We like to "speak softly," but the "big stick" (à la Theodore Roosevelt) of a legally, socially, and morally right cause has to be present and seen to be present and advocated.

Chapter 23

PAPAL AUDIENCES

I remember as a young person the stories of Jean Nussbaum, telling about his audiences with Pope Pius XII. Nussbaum stood out as somewhat of a *héroïque* figure, because he didn't kneel or kiss the pope's ring. Today I know, of course, that kneeling before the pope (much less frequent) and kissing his ring is largely an act of Catholic Church members recognizing the pope's authority as bishop of Rome.

There are three levels of papal audiences: (1) general, often consisting of several thousand people; (2) special, for a relatively small group of people having some special affinity, such as a delegation from some organization; and (3) private, a person or small group, such as a head of a church or government, with or without entourage.

Over the past 45 years I have met the pope a half dozen times, always in the "special" category. The first time was in 1962 in the Sistine Chapel, when Pope John XXIII received a few hundred accredited journalists to Vatican II. I knew there was a certain expectation when the pope came in that journalists would bow and kneel. But I decided (and I was right) that this was for Roman Catholics and others who acknowledge the pope as bishop of Rome and vicar of Christ, but not for me. It was a little awkward, but when you are a Seventh-day Adventist you're used to doing certain things that are different from what the majority or the people in general do, say, eat, wear, or read. Some bowed or knelt. I, with others, remained standing. The pope gave a short speech, and that was it. He was an old man; in fact, he died a few months later.

In 1976 the Conference of Secretaries of Christian World Communions met in Rome, and a small group of a dozen of us was received by Pope Paul VI. We sat in a reception room in the Vatican palace for an hour or so, waiting for the pope to arrive. That's when I noticed an interesting psychology at work.

The pope was completing a general audience in the recently built large audience hall, which holds close to 12,000 people. As we waited, one of the

Vatican officials, usually a bishop, would open the door from time to time and tell us, "The pope is ending his audience." Then: "The pope has left the audience chamber." Then: "The pope is on his way." Finally: "The pope will soon be here."

What was happening, of course, was a building up of expectancy and awe for the occasion. When the pope arrived he walked in very simply, respectfully, and almost with deference.

This impressed the group, of course, and I remember one Protestant general secretary saying to me, "What a saintly man!" It seemed to me a sort of "monarchical simplicity."

In his brief remarks the pope made two observations that were particularly well chosen for the mostly Protestant group of 12 he was meeting with. He said, "There is only one mediator between God and man, Jesus Christ," and "There is only one name under heaven and earth, through which we can have salvation."

He spoke in Italian without notes, though he knew English, because, he said, "I can better express my thoughts in my mother tongue."

After his brief statement he greeted and shook hands with each participant, and gave each of us a souvenir medal. Knowing he would pass out his token of appreciation, I gave him both a General Conference medal as a memento and a book about the Seventh-day Adventist Church and its message. This exchange of souvenir tokens is, of course, not an award, decoration, or badge of merit.

The pope looked at my presentation and said, "Your medal is better than mine!" I felt no inclination to disagree with him. The General Conference souvenir presented the words "Christ our righteousness" and "every eye shall see Him" on one side of the coin. On the other side, the Bible and the Ten Commandments were featured, represented only by Roman numerals, while the fourth commandment was highlighted by the words "Remember the Sabbath day to keep it holy." Thus the presentation revealed both the Adventist and the seventh-day Sabbath message of the Seventh-day Adventist Church. The papal medal represented an artistic portrait of the pope.

From a public relations standpoint, this was a replete success, though a few inside our church were unhappy, because of false information and assuming that the medal was a kind of "medal of honor," rather than two individuals exchanging memory tokens on the occasion of meeting together and simply shaking hands (because this is the way polite human beings greet each other).

Several years later I met Pope John Paul II in connection with the meeting of Secretaries of Christian World Communions. Since I was the secretary, it fell on me to introduce by name each of the two dozen individuals as they met the pope. At this meeting there was much less ceremonial buildup, such as had existed with previous popes.

In 1999 I met the pope in another reception room of the Vatican, the Sala Clementina. This was after the meeting of the Committee Preparing the Millennium Celebration in Rome. I had been invited to represent the Christian World Communions as an advisor. This gave me the opportunity to put in writing two suggestions:

First, Christ should be the center of any Christian millennium celebrations and pilgrimage to Rome. Second, granting indulgences for pilgrim visits to Rome should be avoided.

Coming back to the meeting with the pope: after entering the meeting room, I sat in a seat back in the middle of the hall. I was interested to watch some bishops trying to get seats near the pope, a little like members of the U.S. Congress during the president's State of the Union address reserving seats along the aisle so they can shake his hand and be seen with him on television. An official came and surprised me by inviting me to sit on the front row. In fact, after meeting with a head of state, the pope came into the hall and shook hands with a dozen or so of us on the front row.

This reminded me of Jesus' parable in Luke 14:7-10. Interestingly enough, this same parable was again illustrated for me at the enthronement of the archbishop of Canterbury, George Carey, when one of our group sat on the front row while the rest of us sat in the second and third rows. An Anglican official came and asked him to move back, and he ended up in the fourth row.

The last time I met Pope John Paul II was in 2000, when there was a commemoration at the Colosseum in Rome of the martyrs, Catholic and non-Catholic, of the twentieth century. Again I was asked to represent the Christian World Communions and was one of some 20 people on the platform with the pope. Next to me sat a friend, Bishop Walter Kasper (who recently retired as a cardinal). Unfortunately, there was some rain during the open-air ceremony. When the pope had an umbrella held over him, we also opened the umbrellas we had been given. At one point several of us shook hands with the pope, and most others kissed his ring. All this was a witness before several thousand Roman Catholics looking on and a much larger television audience.

The next day the pope extended an invitation for several of us to have lunch with him at Santa Marta in the Vatican. There were perhaps 40 of us in the dining room. I sat next to the bishop who stands by the papal throne and organizes the papal liturgical functions. He appeared greatly relieved to discover that his American table partner spoke Italian. We had a pleasant, and, for me, enlightening conversation. After lunch the pope gave each of us both a medal and a book on the martyrs of the twentieth century.

I stayed in Santa Marta for several days. This Vatican "hotel" was built several years ago, particularly for guests of the Secretariat of State, and to house the cardinals when they meet for the conclave to elect the next pope. I wonder, *What cardinal occupied my suite for the election of Benedict XVI?*

During my stay it was interesting to walk into the Vatican and be saluted by the Swiss guards in their Michelangelo-inspired uniforms and speak with them in the Swiss-German dialect. Even the smallest of God's servants from time to time enjoys receiving VIP treatment.

Chapter 24

CALENDAR REFORM

Throughout history various calendars have been in use in different parts of the world. Jews, Muslims, Buddhists, and others all have their own calendars.

In the West the two significant calendars in the Christian Era have been the Julian calendar, instituted by Julius Caesar, and, since the sixteenth century, the Gregorian calendar, which we use today. Eastern Orthodox churches still use the Julian calendar. From an Adventist—and biblical—viewpoint the important thing is the orderly continuation of the seven-day weekly cycle, with which the above calendar changes did not interfere. The dates changed, but not the days of the week.

Though the Gregorian calendar was an improvement over what existed before, it does have some problems, such as the fact that months have different lengths, and every four years there is even a leap year with an additional day. Some commercial interests favor a more symmetrical calendar with equal months. Well-meaning people during the twentieth century did, from time to time, advocate reforms of the civil calendar. The problem is that practically all those proposals have one big defect: they break the weekly cycle by introducing one and sometimes even two blank days at the beginning of the year.

Easter and Calendar Reform at Vatican II
The issue came up at the Second Vatican Council. The General Conference asked me, along with Gianfranco Rossi and Jean Nussbaum, to watch and monitor developments in Rome. Together Rossi and I approached various people, including the person responsible for the liturgical calendar of a leading order of the Catholic Church, and Archbishop Bafile (later cardinal), the papal nuncio to the Federal Republic of Germany, the leading Vatican authority regarding the matter of the calendar. Some people don't realize how important Easter is to many denominations. Their church calendar depends on the Easter date. Easter—not

Christmas, as some might think—is the center of their calendar.

We pointed out the problem of any calendar reform breaking the weekly cycle. The Vatican council agreed that any calendar reform of the civil calendar would be acceptable only if it did not disrupt the weekly cycle. Fixing the Easter date (the usual suggestion is the second Sunday after the first Saturday in April) was acceptable as long as there was general agreement among Christian churches.

There are two sequels to the calendar reform issue that came up at Vatican II. As already indicated, fixing the date of Easter, which currently varies up to six weeks from year to year with all the inconveniences this involves, is of interest to many Christian church leaders. Many ecumenical leaders would like to see the Easter date stabilized, with agreement between East and West Christian churches regarding the actual date. The Orthodox Church celebrates Easter usually at a different time from the rest of Christianity, although in 2004 it was on the same date.

WCC, Easter, and Calendar Reform

The World Council of Churches called for a consultation in 1970 at Chambesy, near Geneva. I attended because of the danger of linking Easter to general civil calendar reform. Interestingly, a subcommittee of two people was appointed to draft a statement, the secretary of the archbishop of Canterbury and I. I quickly prepared a draft for consideration, and it was essentially accepted. It affirmed the desirability of any celebration of Easter to be on the same date, suggesting the first Sunday after the first Saturday in April, but stated that this should not be tied to any general calendar reform that broke the continuity of the weekly cycle. Shortly thereafter the Central Committee of the WCC voted to accept this recommendation.

There is an interesting side story to the Chambesy Consultation: The representative of the Greek Orthodox Church was director of the National Observatory of Athens. I had to convince him that any blank day calendar reform breaks the orderly succession of the weekly cycle. He hadn't realized this!

Aleppo Easter Date Consultation

Some 25 years later in 1996 the WCC called a second consultation on the Easter date. I was invited as one of about 15 people, to participate in this meeting. Metropolitan Damaskinos, at that time head of the Orthodox Church in Switzerland, and I played an interesting "historical conscience" role, because we were the only two who had participated in the earlier consultation at Chambesy.

The meeting took place in Aleppo, Syria. Many Christians in the Middle East suffer the problem of various churches in the same area celebrating Easter at different times. Muslims make fun of them, pointing out that Christ "dies and is resurrected," then "dies again and is resurrected once more."

The Aleppo consultation concentrated on the Easter date issue. It confirmed the position that there should be no calendar reform that breaks the weekly cycle and that it was hoped there would be agreement on a common Easter date for Christian churches in both the East and West, in line with previous recommendations pointing to an early April date. This has not happened so far. One of the major obstacles appears to be the rigid tradition of the Russian Orthodox Church.

For me, of course, the issue of general calendar reform had to be watched. The consultation was held in Syria, where we were guests of the Syrian Orthodox Church. Syria was, and I think still is, the only country in the world in which Seventh-day Adventists are specifically banned, and this has been the case for several decades. It was interesting for an Adventist church leader to get an official visa to visit the country. Friends were made, especially with Metropolitan Gregorios Ibrahim, and a year or so later the General Conference of Seventh-day Adventists hosted in the United States a delegation of church leaders headed by Ibrahim from Syria for two weeks, with the hope of working out some cooperative hospital venture in Syria. This is still on the agenda, though it has been delayed for various reasons, not least the war in Iraq and troubles in the Middle East. Metropolitan Ibrahim is still a friend, and is now a member of the International Religious Liberty Association Committee of Experts.

God works in mysterious ways, connecting past contacts through bridge building to the present.

Chapter 25

INTERCHURCH RELATIONS

With the passing of time, especially when stepping down after 15 years as director of the General Conference Department of Public Affairs and Religious Liberty in 1995, my responsibilities during the next decade concentrated more and more on leadership for the General Conference in interchurch relations. This is a somewhat controversial area, especially for some individuals on the borders of the church. They seem to spend much time criticizing the Adventist Church and other denominations. They only see evil outside, and frequently inside the church, as well.

My interest in interchurch relations grew gradually. I was thrown into this worldwide phenomenon not by my own choosing. But by being asked to represent the church at the Second Vatican Council in 1962, I came to realize that the ecumenical phenomenon, and dealing with other churches, was something Adventists could no longer ignore, in part because of exponential church growth. I remember reading about some discussions that were had subsequent to the Adventist Church passing the membership mark of 144,000. A church representing much more than 20 million people can't just hide its head in the sand of isolation and act as if no one else exists, or at most only has value as an object of aggressive evangelistic persuasion.

There are wonderful, faithful Christians across the ecclesiastical spectrum. A number of whom have become devoted friends; some have passed away, but I expect to see them on the great resurrection morning. This in no way diminishes Adventists' special responsibility to present the eternal gospel and prepare people to meet the soon-coming Lord.

Observing other religious bodies and attending some of their meetings helps Adventists to know what is happening in the religious world, gives us the opportunity to react and make our viewpoints known, and report back to our church. Ignorance of what goes on outside our denominational borders is not bliss. Furthermore, it is almost unbelievable how many erroneous concepts about Adventism float around in both church and secular circles.

A leading Baptist theologian told me one day, "Your name is Seventh-day Adventist. This means that you believe Christ will return on the Sabbath!" Other Christians think we believe in salvation by works, especially by keeping the Sabbath. Some of those ideas probably came from some legalistic offshoots. Sitting in pharisaic isolation does little to represent or promote the church and its teachings.

Refusing to meet with other people and not representing our viewpoint is seen as a mark of ignorant sectarianism. To use an analogy from sports, we have to be on the religious playing field and hit some theological home runs, or at least kick some field goals in Christian service and human relations. Opting out and not playing at all is tantamount to forfeiting the religious game by default.

When I came to the General Conference in 1980, I got the GC to establish the Council on Interchurch/Interfaith Relations. We needed some kind of body we could go to, that was larger than PARL and more representative. PARL is broad enough for government relations, but when it comes to other churches and theological conversations, we need the Biblical Research Institute involved; we need the *Adventist Review,* the Ministerial Association, and theologians from Andrews University. We need good scholars, conservative theologians, yet not the "I know everything and I have to convert you" kind. This is not the first purpose of dialogue, which is reaching "understanding."

As a result of our endeavors, the church is now respected and even held in esteem by many other religious bodies on the international level. The situation locally, though influenced positively by what happens in the worldwide circles, varies considerably and depends to a large extent on our local knowledge, sensitivity, openness, involvement, and competence in witness and bridge building.

Dialogue and Conversations

Over the years I have led out in conversations (shorter and less structured) and dialogues (longer and more organized) between Adventists and other religious bodies. This has been an exciting learning curve and witnessing experience. I thank God and the leadership of my church for this experience.

The first conversation was an informal, then semiformal, get-together on an annual basis for several years around 1970 with the World Council of Churches in Geneva and at Collonges Adventist Seminary, a few miles from Geneva, just across the border in France. This was a useful meeting. My friend, Lukas Vischer, was the leader from the WCC side. The discussions and results were summarized in a booklet put out by the WCC entitled *So Much in Common* (a title chosen by the WCC). These meetings were significant. They have been criticized on occasion by some from both sides, but for opposite reasons. The conversations informed the religious world that although Adventists were not going to join the WCC, they are to be taken seriously as a Bible- and Christ-centered church.

A Flagship Dialogue

A substantial dialogue over four years took place with the Lutheran World Federation (1994-1998). The papers and results have been published in a fine book, *Lutherans and Adventists in Conversation*. I consider these meetings a great success. Adventists see themselves in many ways as "children" of Luther, the great Reformer. We were seen by our Lutheran partners not as a sect, but a free denomination or church. Some Lutheran hard-liners in Germany have been unwilling to accept these results as yet, and have asked for further conversations.

In the meantime, some see Adventists as a *Sondergemeinschaft*, sort of a "special religious fellowship," something between a church and a sect. I regret this "state church" mentality, which I hope will, in due course, be replaced by more typical Lutheran justice and justification by faith, not theological prejudice. There's still a lot of fence mending and bridge building to do. I pay tribute to the wonderful Lutheran theologians we met and who gained our lasting respect.

We also had a one week dialogue with the World Alliance of Reformed Churches (WARC). The conversations were somewhat limited by the parameters set by the WARC theology department. We met with gifted theologians and covered quite a bit of material, but I hope we can broaden the scope of this dialogue in the future.

In the meantime, a dialogue is going on with the Presbyterian Church (USA), with John Graz and William Johnsson taking the lead. I am just a consultant.

Recently John Graz led out in launching a dialogue/conversation with the Mennonite World Conference, with William Johnsson chairing the meeting for the Adventists. In the past I usually assigned papers to others, but now I had to prepare a paper about Seventh-day Adventist ecclesiology and church organization. The meeting was a spiritual treat, and showed how much we owe to the Anabaptist movement. We are children not only of the Reformation but also of what is called the Radical Reformation, which among several other things supported separation of church and state and believer's baptism. I hope this dialogue will continue in due course in another meeting with our Mennonite friends.

Conversations With the Orthodox Ecumenical Patriarchate

Together with John Graz, I was involved in breaking the ice, so to speak, and starting "pre-conversations" over two days with leaders of the Ecumenical Patriarchate of Constantinople in Istanbul. These conversations are still on hold, waiting for a suitable time to proceed. While the Ecumenical Patriarch is the spiritual leader of the Eastern Orthodox communion, and thus from an historical viewpoint this Patriarchate is very important, the staff in Istanbul and available theological dialogue partners is somewhat limited. While conversations with Adventists are seen as "desirable," they are not viewed as a priority.

Dialogue With Sabbathkeeping Christian Churches

I also initiated dialogues with Sabbathkeeping Christian groups, particularly the Church of God (Seventh Day) and the Worldwide Church of God. The latter church, after the death of its founder, the dynamic but controversial Herbert Armstrong, moved in a radically different theological direction. Some of the changes are to be strongly commended, though unfortunately the biblical seventh-day Sabbath has been considerably deemphasized (some would say "given up"). Several apparently competing groups have now emerged, with the remaining church core having sold its valuable property in Pasadena and moved to Glendora, California.

Contacts With Seventh Day Baptists

I had several friendly contacts with Seventh Day Baptists. For many years their central office sent observers to our General Conference sessions. I attended some of their meetings and was always well received.

At one of their sessions I suggested to their ecumenical committee that a statement they had written years earlier outlining the differences between Seventh Day Baptists and Seventh-day Adventists be looked at by a joint committee. This suggestion was accepted by the committee, but after I left and the matter was placed before the session, it was turned down. I was never told why. I have a sense that they were likely more comfortable with a description of Seventh-day Adventist beliefs written by themselves alone, in which Seventh-day Adventists do not recognize themselves because of the tendentious and inexact representations.

It's too bad. In this case, for the time being, old bias seems to have won out over fairness and accuracy.

As a result of several frank and positive contacts, there has been a noticeable decline in any hostile polemics and backbiting between Sabbathkeeping groups.

Conversations With Christ's Other Followers

A more recent theological dialogue has been with the Salvation Army, this highly respected and devoted church that serves sacrificially many who others overlook or neglect.

The conversations were started in England in 1979 and 1980 by Commissioner Harry Williams and myself. He became a dear friend. He was not only a top leader of the Salvation Army, but also a distinguished plastic surgeon and received the Order of the British Empire.

After I moved to Washington and he retired, the conversations were temporarily placed on the back burner. Then they were revived with new vigor, concluding for the present with dialogue meetings in Canada and Washington. There was much agreement and cordial Christian fellowship. As I write these lines one of the leading Salvation Army participants in the conversations, Commissioner Linda Bond, has been elected Salvation Army general.

We have also had informal conversations in Geneva with some Catholic theologians, covering such topics as Sabbath versus Sunday, the approach to Scripture, and discussion of the Seventh-day Adventists' 28 fundamental beliefs.

All these conversations clarify our position, increase mutual understanding of each other, and help remove false stereotypes and misunderstandings. The conversations in which I have been involved have not only increased my knowledge of the doctrines and position of our dialogue partners, but have also enlarged my understanding of the teachings of *my* church and increased my faith in the beliefs and organization of this church I love and serve, as did my parents, and my father's parents.

It's a good feeling to know that interchurch affairs and relations are in the competent hands of dedicated thinkers and administrators, such as John Graz, William Johnsson, Ganoune Diop (a rising star), leaders in the Biblical Research Institute, and other scholars, such as Denis Fortin, dean of the Seventh-day Adventist Theological Seminary, who will carry things to greater heights and the inevitable triumph of God's kingdom.

In all these endeavors I have been grateful for the understanding and, when needed, support of General Conference and division leadership. President Neal Wilson saw the need for careful theological engagement. President Jan Paulsen, himself a trained theologian and missiologist, greatly contributed to the Seventh-day Adventist-Lutheran conversations. President Robert Folkenberg showed his interest by attending a portion of these conversations in Geneva. President Robert Pierson joined me for a brief courtesy visit to the World Council of Churches headquarters and met its general secretary, Eugene Carson Blake.

Chapter 26

A HALF CENTURY OF VISITS TO POLAND

The year 2011 marked the fiftieth anniversary of my first visit to Poland in 1961. I usually went to Poland by traveling east from Western Europe. But for my first visit I traveled west by train from Moscow. As the division education director, I had been visiting schools in Scandinavia and Finland with Richard Hammill, then associate director of the General Conference Education Department. We decided to go to Warsaw to visit the Adventist school at Podkowa Lesna, going by train from Finland via St. Petersburg (then Leningrad) and Moscow.

The leaders of the Polish Union were at the station to welcome us. This was the beginning of decades of most fruitful contacts in Poland, not only with the leadership and members of the Polish Seventh-day Adventist Church, but with government officials, cultural voices, religious leaders of other Christian churches in Poland, as well as a few non-Christian religious leaders. Some of the key purposes were always to improve interchurch relations and religious liberty, and to strengthen the image and outreach of the Adventist Church.

The early contacts in the sixties were not easy. Communism was at its zenith in Poland. Conversations with government officials, while always polite, could be a little tense and challenging. I always spoke honestly with government officials. I didn't, of course, tell them everything that passed through my mind; but what I said was factual and represented the true outlook and position of the church.

The first director of the government Religious Affairs office that I met was Minister Skarzinski. I believe he had previously been minister of culture. He was a relatively hard-liner insofar as the Communist Party was concerned. He attacked the United States regarding Vietnam. He said, "It is very clear who is wrong when a robber attacks a widow."

My answer: "You first have to decide who is the robber and who is the widow!"

From February 4 through 7, 2001, I visited Poland and had a number of positive and pleasant contacts. It was sort of a commemorative trip, in which we looked back over decades of contacts. Together with the leadership of the Polish Union Conference (W. Polok, president; Z. Lyko, secretary; and R. Chalupka, communications director), I met Minister Duresz, head of the Polish president's office (President Kwasniewski was not in Warsaw), and we had the opportunity of acquainting the minister with the work of the Adventist Church. I also met Metropolitan Sawa, head of the Orthodox Church, a longtime friend of the Adventist Church, whom I had known for a number of years, as I did his predecessor, the late Metropolitan Basili, who had honored me with the Order of Mary Magdalene. This is an interesting story in itself:

My father was with me on a visit to Metropolitan Basili. I was supposed to receive the Order on that occasion, but he was so impressed by my father that he asked if I would mind if he gave the Order to my father (the Metropolitan had only one medal and authenticity certificate ready at the time), and he would invest me with the Order on my next visit, which he subsequently did.

Visit to General Jaruzelski

Two events especially stood out in connection with the April 2001 visit. I paid a courtesy call on the former president of Poland, General Wojciech Jaruzelski. Like former presidents of the United States, Jaruzelski was provided with a suite of offices and security protection. He was now in his middle 70s. It was during his presidency that the Solidarity movement came to the fore, and strong efforts were made to throw off the "Communist yoke." There was civil unrest, strikes, and warnings from Moscow that things were going too far. Jaruzelski proclaimed martial law and clamped down on the Solidarity movement, which was led by Lech Walesa, who later became president of Poland. (I remember being a special guest of the government when Walesa spoke on the Polish Independence Day.)

Churches, however, were left to carry on with their normal religious activities. I was able to freely visit Poland during the time of marshal law without any particular problems. I even visited the main Solidarity office in Warsaw.

Jaruzelski has been criticized heavily for putting the brakes on the pro-democracy and freedom forces. However, in my limited judgment some such intervention was probably necessary, because the U.S.S.R. was not yet ready to accept a new democratic regime and would have probably invaded Poland (as it did in Czechoslovakia in 1968 during the "Prague Spring"; and earlier in Hungary). The Poles would likely have resisted, and there could very well have been a bloodbath.

I found Jaruzelski a humble man (his office was simple, even austere), willing to admit that he'd made mistakes. He seemed interested in the needs of poor people and in the activities of the Adventist Church in Polish society. He gave evidence of being a Polish patriot and awaits, one would hope, a balanced verdict from history.

Polish Bible Society Contacts

The second, somewhat nostalgic event was a meeting at the Polish Bible Society. When I first visited this organization in 1961, it was called the British and Foreign Bible Society in Poland. The director was Mr. Alexander Enholc, and we became friends, though he died a few years later. His daughter, Barbara Narzynska, followed him as director, and is a well-known figure not only in Poland, but also in Bible Society and religious circles outside Poland.

We have been good friends for some 50 years. During this meeting we looked back over four decades of contacts, and I was surprised—and touched—by the extent they appreciated our past relationship in favor of the Bible work in Poland and church work in general. We recalled that in the sixties I carried with me documents to the British and Foreign Bible Society in London that the Bible Society didn't particularly want to send by mail. The contacts helped open the way for our church to be deeply involved, not only in the Bible Society in Poland in general, but specifically in Bible translation to the point that Z. Lyko, secretary of the Polish Union Conference, for some time chaired the committee supervising the translation of the Old Testament into modern Polish (the New Testament had already been completed). I was surprised to hear that I was to join a select group of "honorary members" of the Polish Bible Society.

In fact, some months later Narzynska took the trouble of traveling several hours all the way to Gdynia and Gdansk to meet me. I was with my wife, John and Medina Graz, and some friends from the American Religious Town Hall on a Baltic cruise, which had stopped for the day at Gdynia. She gave a dinner in my honor and presented me with a beautifully prepared certificate, which I prize, making me an honorary member of the Bible Society. I was astonished to hear that the previous recipient was Patriarch Bartholomew of Constantinople.

For several years the presiding bishop of the Lutheran Church in Poland happened to be Narzynska's husband. At the Bible Society meeting he spoke most eloquently about our contacts over decades. He stated that for them in Poland for many years, I represented the image of the worldwide Seventh-day Adventist Church and that this was of considerable encouragement in those years when internal pressures and isolation were discouraging factors. These visits from abroad upheld international fellowship, optimism, and religious liberty.

Significant Individuals From the Past

I also visited two individuals from past leadership who have made a significant contribution to the Adventist Church. It is easy to forget people who are no longer in office. That is a human tendency, even in the church. If I have one little quality, it is to remember past friends; once a friend, always a friend.

Adam Lopatka was for several years minister for Religious Affairs and then chief justice of the Polish Supreme Court. Though a Communist, he was in many ways open and helpful to the Adventist Church. This should not be forgotten.

Jan Wisniewski was involved in our Polish Publishing House for many years as director of the bindery, and was especially successful in getting paper when it was very difficult to obtain. Though not a baptized Adventist, he fully cooperated with the church and gave excellent leadership. I visited these two old friends with pleasure and expressed appreciation for their past help and support. Adam Lopatka has since died, and Jan Wisniewski retired in 2004.

Strong Leadership in Intricate Times

Over these past decades the Adventist Church in Poland has had strong and capable leadership. Of course, none of us is perfect, but God uses our gifts, adds to them, and forgives our mistakes. Stanislaw Dabrowski was a key player in the leadership of the Adventist Church in Poland for some 30 years, including 24 years as president. It was a difficult task to be steady and evenhanded and lead the church in those years soon after World War II. These were tough times politically and economically. He had to navigate many problems, but he was a strong man with a supporting business and financial background.

The church had been divided, and Dabrowski helped bring the two factions together. He led out in making our church a respected religious body, both vis-à-vis the government and other churches. During his administration the church moved from the level of an inconsequential and marginalized sect, to a recognized and significant church. The Polish Parliament even passed a special law recognizing the status of our church and its relationship to the state. When he stepped down as leader of the church, it was both for him and other leaders a traumatic experience. His distinct contributions can never be overlooked and should never be undervalued.

A close collaborator during these many years was Zachariasz Lyko. I have sometimes jokingly referred to him as the Talleyrand of the Seventh-day Adventist Church in Poland. It made no difference who was running the church—Lyko was closely involved in or with the leadership. His legal mind, theological acumen, skills as a writer, and matchless gifts in dealing with government and non-Adventist church officials have been invaluable to both the church and the Protestant and Orthodox Christian Theological Academy. He became the first (and so far only) Seventh-day Adventist to hold professorial rank granted by government appointment at the academy. He was a prolific writer in Polish. He wrote many of the books our church published in Poland. Unfortunately, he died unexpectedly in 2010 leaving a difficult void to fill, and for me a lonesome spot against the Polish sky. We had done so many things together.

In more recent years, men like Wladyslaw Polok and Pavel Lazar have successfully picked up the mantle of leadership and kept the church's ship on an even keel, sailing ahead, and opening the way for the work of their colleagues and successors.

Chapter 27

CLUBS AND ASSOCIATIONS— UNEXPECTED FALLOUT

One of the most prestigious clubs in the United States is the Cosmos Club in Washington, D.C., founded in 1878 as a men's club in the British-London tradition. Today both men and women who are regarded as "eminent in their profession," or have made a "meritorious contribution to human knowledge," are accepted as members.

After arriving in Washington in the summer of 1980 to work at the General Conference, I checked around to see how to best obtain contacts and information to support me in my work for public affairs. I decided three organizations would be useful to belong to, if possible: (1) Rotary Club, (2) National Press Club, (3) Cosmos Club. The first two sounded feasible; the last seemed definitely a very long shot.

Rotary Membership

Fortunately, friend of longstanding and esteemed colleague, Charles Hirsch, was a member of the Silver Spring Rotary Club and proposed me for membership. Rotary is the senior and worldwide service club. This gave me an introduction to the local business and professional community.

One useful result was that when we wanted to build the new General Conference headquarters, the Montgomery County executive, Sid Kramer, was a member of Rotary and friend, and we still are. In fact, he was club president when I was inducted in the summer of 1980. When we ran into some serious opposition from Montgomery County that threatened to torpedo the building project, my contact with him helped clear the way.

I have now been a member of Rotary for more than 30 years, have served as both secretary and president, and made a number of friends. Rotary's motto, "Service Above Self," is truly Christian in essence. Every Rotarian is expected to ask a four-way test before he or she acts: 1. Is it the truth? 2. Is it fair to all concerned? 3. Will it build goodwill and better friendships? 4. Will it be beneficial to all concerned? My life is influenced by these questions.

I joined the National Press Club with the help of Ernest Steed, a close friend in the International Commission for the Prevention of Alcoholism and Drug Dependency (ICPA) when he was executive director and I was a vice president. Since then I have been president for a number of years. Steed was one of the greatest "promoters" in the Seventh-day Adventist Church, the proverbial person who could "sell ice to Eskimos." He could move in where most of us would hesitate for fear of embarrassment.

The Cosmos Club—The Christian Connection

Joining the Cosmos Club was a whole different ball game. I had no idea how to get in, or whether I was even eligible for membership. An Adventist, as far as I knew, had never gotten into this establishment bastion. Again, providence opened the door.

I had mentioned my desire to be a member of the Cosmos Club to a family friend, DeWitt Fox, a neurosurgeon and former editor of *Life and Health*, who belonged to a number of clubs in Los Angeles. He and his wife, Pinki, were close friends with my sister Colette and her surgeon husband, Charles. Fox and his wife went on a cruise and met William Barton, former chief counsel of the United States Chamber of Commerce. In conversation at a table in the ship's dining room, Barton mentioned that he was a member of the Cosmos Club. Fox immediately chimed in by saying he had a friend in Washington who would make a good member! Barton, a devout Methodist, had helped organize a prayer breakfast at the Cosmos Club. And that, no doubt, was a factor in his willingness to sponsor me, a fellow Christian, for membership.

Soon Barton called me unexpectedly, invited me for lunch at the Cosmos Club, and introduced me to a couple members. After showing me some of the architectural splendors of the building where the club meets, he handed me a book with the names of all the members and asked me to find some names of members who would be willing to support my nomination. That was a humiliating experience for me, for out of more than 3,000 names from all over the United States and other countries in the club register, I knew practically no one! Fortunately, Barton agreed to be my sponsor and get a couple of his friends to support my nomination.

I had met James Matthews, the Methodist bishop of Washington and a well-known leader of Methodism, in Geneva at meetings of the Central Committee of the World Council of Churches, but I felt he probably wouldn't remember me. So I got a close friend, Joe Hale, general secretary of the World Methodist Council, to contact the bishop. Matthews then called and invited me to the Cosmos Club and treated me as an old friend! His wife is the daughter of E. Stanley Jones, the famous missionary to India, and author of *The Christ of the Indian Road*. He agreed to be my cosponsor.

Several members and nonmembers wrote letters of support, including Ambassador Max Kampelman, who, at my invitation, had spoken at the Rome Religious Liberty World Congress. He had been chief United States negotiator in the Strategic Arms Reduction Talks in Geneva and received the Presidential Medal of Freedom. Several general secretaries of Christian World Communion wrote letters of support, as did several Cosmos club members. George T. Harding, my close friend from Pacific Union College days, wrote to two psychiatrists who were members of the Cosmos Club, and they supported my candidacy after meeting me. It's great to have loyal and eminent friends and see how God opens doors that seemed nonexistent or closed.

The Cosmos Club has a membership committee of 11 members. If two vote against you, you don't get in. Somehow I slipped under the bar, have enjoyed membership for more than 25 years, and have served on several committees. The Cosmos Club membership has been an asset to the General Conference for protocol purposes. Luncheons, dinners, or meetings with important guests of the General Conference have taken place, and leading personalities have been able to stay in this prestigious club in my name as guests of the General Conference.

Adventist Bridge Builders

Seventh-day Adventists have been involved in a number of bridge building organizations that reach out to society in creative leadership at arm's length from the church. I have had the satisfaction, and also the pleasure for many years, of being involved in especially two.

One of them is the International Commission for the Prevention of Alcoholism and Drug Dependency (ICPA). The ICPA was the brainchild of W. A. Scharffenberg, who wanted to emphasize prevention, not just cure. He gathered around him some outstanding people, such as Andrew Ivy, vice president of the University of Illinois at Chicago; Winton Beaven, college and university administrator and consummate lecturer; and Charles Watson, a church diplomat as smooth as silk.

Scharffenberg's successor as executive director of the ICPA, Ernest Steed, was a tremendous and tireless promoter. Peter Landless, the current executive director, has lifted the ICPA out of temporary doldrums to new heights. It has been my privilege and honor to serve the ICPA, first as director of the European region, then as vice president, and now for more than a dozen years as president and board chair.

American Religious Town Hall: Beaming Brotherhood

The second organization is the American Religious Town Hall Meeting and telecast. This was the creation of a Seventh-day Adventist minister, Albert Leiske, large city evangelist, pastor, and, for a time, hospital administrator.

While serving as pastor in St. Paul, Minnesota, Leiske felt a call from God, starting with a dream and his praying and thinking about how to expand and enlarge his Christian ministry. He felt strongly that God's answer was to start a public roundtable discussion on television between ministers of different denominations or religions, promoting open and frank back and forth interchanges. These would at times deal with touchy issues, but always with respect and without rancor, ever upholding and promoting civil and religious freedom. The program began in St. Paul in 1952, but very soon it went nationwide over many stations, and has continued without interruption since. The telecast has been a great success. It has been aired on Hope Channel and now the Internet.

In the early eighties I was approached about being a panelist, and have now been a participant for 30 years!

My first contact with Bishop Leiske, as the founding panelists insisted he be called, illustrates his decisive and goal-oriented personality. I called him on the phone, told him when I planned to arrive, and asked whether someone would be meeting me at the Dallas Airport. He answered, "Well, aren't you coming to meet friends?"

"Well, yes," I said.

"Well, then," he said categorically, "if nobody's there to meet you at the airport, if I were you I'd simply grab the next plane and fly home!" Quite a character!

Supporting such a large and growing nondenominational television ministry became an increasingly heavy financial burden. Airtime and studio production have become increasingly expensive. The solution he and his son, Robert, found was buying, building, and operating a nonprofit chain of nursing and related health-care facilities with a religious orientation and thereby supporting the telecast. When Albert Leiske died in 1984, his son Robert took over leadership. When Robert died 20 years later, Robert's wife, Elizabeth, became CEO. Both Robert and Elizabeth continued to be great supporters of the television ministry. She has dedicated her life, and much of the organization's funds, to supporting the telecast, which was the original historical reason for founding the American

Religious Town Hall. She is always present when the programs are recorded, and gives meticulous care to its budget and financial needs.

It has been my responsibility, as editorial director, for the past 20 or more years to choose the topics and prepare the introductory moderator's statement for each program. I'm now approaching the 1,000 mark of the number of topics written for the panelists to freely discuss. It has been no small task to come up with a new and, hopefully, interesting topic for every week of the year, but it is an exciting and fulfilling activity, not least in retirement. As panelists we have become good friends, not always in agreement, but always in exercising the intrinsic American right to express honest opinions. Unfortunately, all the original panelists have now passed away, and some of their replacements have also died. I knew them all, with the exception of one. Excellent new panelists have filled the vacant spots. The current moderator is my pastor at the Spencerville church in Maryland, Jerry Lutz. He does an excellent job, and it is a joy to work with him. God has blessed our efforts and association together. Bridges of understanding and generosity of spirit have been constructed.

I am both grateful and quietly proud to be part of these two witness and bridge-building organizations.

Chapter 28

WRITER *MALGRÉ LUI*

I became known in Seventh-day Adventist circles, to a large extent, through my writings. Before my mid-30s I would never have imagined this.

I liked preaching, teaching, lecturing, committee discussions, but not writing. I've always found writing hard work. I remember one occasion in 1962 when I was writing articles for the *Adventist Review* about the Second Vatican Council. After I turned in my first article for each of the four yearly sessions, I was then expected to write a weekly article for the next eight weeks or so.

One week during the first session I just could not, for several days, come up with the expected article. I was greatly distressed and literally had tears in my eyes! Finally, with the Lord's help, a creative flash of inspiration struck, and the article emerged.

Prior to the assignment to cover Vatican II for *Adventist Review*, I had written only sporadically, though as a student at Pacific Union College I had served as a reporter and managing editor of the *Campus Chronicle*. I attended and reported about some campaign presentations by President Truman, Governor Dewey, and Henry Wallace. Some of my articles appeared in church publications in Italy, France, and Britain, but the real surge forward dates from Vatican II and the three dozen articles that appeared in *Adventist Review* and several other publications.

Since then I have written in a score of publications, Adventist as well as non-Adventist.

I should've been aware that the gift of writing was somehow present in the Beach family. My great-grandfather David Beach was a newspaper editor in Canada before his early death in his 40s. My father wrote several books, one of which was a best seller in a half dozen or more languages, particularly in French, for which he took no royalties for years. My mother had a natural gift for writing and storytelling. But living nearly 30 years in non-English-speaking countries, with three lively children to raise, she was hindered from reaching her full literary potential. My sister Jo Ray has been a bright star on the book writing firmament, with some dozen published college textbooks, including two best sellers. She writes under the name McCuen. While Jo Ray can sit at her computer and easily, it seems, pour out an article, play, or book chapter, I have to plod along laboriously, writing, changing, and rewriting.

My familiarity with several languages has complicated things, but has also helped considerably to enlarge my vocabulary (but not improve my spelling!).

My first book was *Vatican II: Bridging the Abyss* (1968), which analyzed theological and other developments in the Roman Catholic Church from an Adventist perspective. The book was also published in Polish.

My second book, *Ecumenism: Boon or Bane?* (1974), analyzed the ecumenical movement, pointing out its fortes, but also quite candidly its weak points. At the Lambeth Conference in 1978, the archbishop of Canterbury, Donald Coggan, referred in conversation to it. The book was also translated and published in Germany, Denmark, Netherlands, Finland, Croatia (a revised and updated version) and extracts in other languages (e.g., Korean).

Pattern for Progress (1985), an analysis of church organization and its meaning, was written with my father, Walter R. Beach, and was given by the General Conference to all the delegates at the 1985 General Conference session in New Orleans. Various extracts have appeared in other languages and on CD in Germany.

Bright Candle of Courage (1989) discusses religious liberty as a principle and in various historical settings. It was translated into Spanish.

The variety and scope of my writing interests is further seen in the book I wrote describing my visits to some 100 Rotary Clubs around the world with the spinning title, *Rotating the World With Rotary* (1990). (*The Rotarian*, the Rotary International magazine, gave the book a short review.)

My most recent book, jointly written with John Graz, my friend and successor as head of the Public Affairs and Religious Liberty Department for the Adventist Church, is *101 Questions Adventists Ask* (2000). The book covers a gamut of questions of interest to Adventists and non-Adventists. The book has been translated into French, German, Polish, and Spanish.

Over the years I've authored several hundred articles, ranging from travelogues to in-depth theological discussion. Few are aware that I authored quite a number of General Conference position statements voted by ADCOM, the Executive Committee, Annual Councils, or released at

General Conference sessions. The breadth of my interests and expertise (I hope) is seen in the fact I authored the *General Conference Rules of Order* (with the support of General Conference counsel Walter Carson and Todd McFarland regarding occasional minor revisions).

I have also been a contributor to several encyclopedias, dictionaries, and other books, and have edited or helped edit several books. For many years it has been my responsibility to write the moderator's statements for the weekly telecast of the American Religious Townhall.

Practice Makes Proficient

Having taken but two English classes in the U.S., I tell the many people for whom English is not a first language, but who still have to write in English, that they have every hope of becoming good writers. While writing involves hard work, persistence bears fruit. The more you write, the more you grow, and writing becomes easier. As you work at it, your pen will flow more smoothly and your computer will produce better and more polished prose. Be of good cheer. There is a writer in many of you, and the God-given gift may simply be waiting to be awakened, nurtured, and revealed.

Some Caution

A word of caution: Think about what you are writing and the views or opinions you are planning to express. Writing is not a judicious way to let off steam. I have read some nonsensical, false, and even vicious things people have written. Oral presentations can be more casual, and you can often explain what you said or even "explain away" what you should not have said. However, what is printed, although not quite etched on stone, is nevertheless written for everyone to see. Remember: Writers are the only people who actually publish their mistakes!

Fortunately, most editors can improve or even correct what you write before publication. I remember a colleague who was displeased if an editor changed anything in an article he had written. My experience, for which I am grateful, is that at least 90 percent of what editors changed in my writing was an improvement, or made the article fit into the available space. Therefore, I've received considerable satisfaction in reading something I wrote 10, 25, or even 50 years ago, and discover it has stood the test of time and does not embarrass me now!

Some people like to write about only one subject. This reminds me of the refutable saying that there are two kinds of preachers: those who preach the same sermon, but change biblical texts, and those that use the same text, but preach different sermons! Looking back over a half century of writing hundreds of articles, papers, and six books, I find, as a friend recently pointed out, an unexpectedly broad range of topics: travel, theology, history, religious liberty, church-state issues, Sabbath school, social and political responsibility, spiritual edification, Christian education, ecumenical issues and trends, statements by the church. All this probably makes me a jack of all writing trades and master of none.

On the other hand, I've enjoyed being a generalist and "popularizer" of scholarship, even thoughts originating in other minds, rather than one who specializes in less and less, until he knows very deeply everything about almost nothing!

PART III:
THINKING

"Strong minds are needed. The human intellect must gain expansion and vigor. . . . Brain power . . . must be put to the stretch, to solve hard problems and master them"
—Ellen G. White, *Fundamentals of Christian Education*, p. 226

"But we desire to hear of thee [Paul] what thou thinkest" (Acts 28:22).

Chapter 29

BRIDGE BUILDING: A LIFE WORK OF HOPE

For years I have worked to build bridges of understanding, mutual respect, and conscientious cooperation, where this seemed both feasible and advisable, between individuals and church organizations. I wanted others to view Seventh-day Adventists and my church as Christ- and Bible-centered, as a people with a social conscience of service and upholding freedom of religion and belief, not only for themselves, but for all.

This is not a timed program of quick and all-out promotion, but a thoughtful, and seemingly agonizingly slow and timeless process of public affairs, conversation, dialogue, and living by example. It takes time to build confidence and bridges of communication, especially where and when suspicion and false stereotypes have dominated personal and interchurch relations.

However, reckless and thoughtless people, often on the fringes or out of the church, see themselves as religious saboteurs, whose task is simply to blow up bridges of contact and goodwill. Anyone can, with vapidity of mind, blow up a bridge in a few seconds, but it takes thoughtful, prudent, and deliberate effort to build a bridge between formerly indifferent and perhaps even hostile individuals or communities. It takes bridges to bring together the scattered and faithful remnant.

Some Christians have a fortress mentality. They love living safely in a "fortress," secure and well separated from the surrounding world by a doctrinal and cultural moat. Perhaps once a year they organize a quick sortie. They lower the rusty drawbridge and march out in an "evangelistic campaign" and gather as many "prisoners" as possible. After completing the raid, they rush back into the fortress, lift the drawbridge, and feel safe and comfortable again.

Of course, what I have just written is metaphorical, but you surely get the point! We need open bridges, used bridges, to proclaim the "eternal gospel" and finish the work. When the kingdom's gospel of salvation is "preached in all the world," using all available bridging links, "then shall the end come" (Matt. 24:14). This is the promise of Jesus; this is my invincible hope.

Chapter 30

THE ADVENTIST CHRISTIAN AND POLITICS

While director of PARL I was often asked about Christian involvement in politics. It is an old and complicated story with a long history, much of it scandalous, even oppressive. Interestingly, Jesus said little about political society. He presented no sociopolitical platform and rejected any zealot-type kingship. He made it clear that His kingdom is essentially not of this world.

However, it must be true that His teachings will have a socioeconomic fallout. He presented the messianic task as spiritual good news that clearly included a social dimension of good news for those who are poor, blind, oppressed. Thus a Christian will have a sociopolitical outlook and responsibility vis-à-vis fellow human beings. A passage in Jeremiah has intrigued me. The prophet sends a message from God to the exiled Jewish population in Babylon in order to counteract the leaders and false prophets who were telling the people not to help build up society in Babylon. Speaking for the Lord, Jeremiah encouraged the people to "seek the peace and prosperity of the city to which I have carried you into exile. Pray to the Lord for it, because if it prospers, you too will prosper" (Jer. 29:7, NIV).

There seems here an obvious call to take sincere responsibility for the sociopolitical society in which we live and make a prayerful and productive contribution to the surrounding community, rather than opting out by exhibiting a negative and sterile isolationism.

Today increasing numbers of Adventists hold or have held political office, up to and including head of government or state. This is especially understandable in countries where a relatively sizeable percentage of the population is made up of Seventh-day Adventists.

The task of any Adventist in political leadership will not be easy. Joseph, Daniel, and Ezra didn't have smooth sailing. Neither did Ugandan prime minister Samson Kisekka. The dangers and temptations of political life are legion. Politics is often the art of compromise. Self-promotion is the order of the political day.

Nevertheless, there are great opportunities. Ellen G. White affirmed that there is nothing wrong in young people aspiring to make laws and sitting and taking part in legislative halls. If someone feels called to go into politics and elective government service, we should not automatically stand in the way. I encourage young people to aim high, but we have to warn them of the possible dangers and pitfalls that lie ahead.

On the other hand, pastors and teachers in our schools should always be guarded and carefully avoid getting involved in party politics. This can be divisive for the church. Furthermore, there is the danger of politics becoming a hard and demanding taskmaster, absorbing all a person's time and trouble.

Evangelism or Service?

Evangelism and service are both important aspects of God's mission in this world. They should not work in opposition to each other. We have to proclaim both God's salvific *love*, which is the core of evangelism, and God's *will*, which involves both belief and service. We must value both evangelism and service. They both involve "doing."

Some see service, or social action, as simply a part of evangelism or as a means of "preevangelism." Such an approach to evangelism can be misunderstood and seen as cunning or even deceitful. I would tend to see evangelism and service as two separate, or, in the words of the late John Stott, "parallel tracks" of God's mission. Though they support each other, they are separate aspects of the mission God has entrusted to His disciples and church. While, indeed, evangelism must ever be the overarching responsibility, the immediate priority may differ.

This is well illustrated in the New Testament story of the wounded and robbed man on the Jericho road. What was his first need? Was it a Bible study? Hardly—it was to receive medical care. Later, during another visit, the priority could change. The good Samaritan did promise to visit the wounded man.

Chapter 31

A CHANGING CHURCH

I've spent more than threescore and 10 years actively serving the Seventh-day Adventist Church, and I've been privy to a lot of change.

An obvious change is the sheer size and extension of the church. Adventists now have work in more than 200 countries. In some of these countries Adventists are a large religio-social force to be reckoned with.

When I was a child, it could be said that our church was largely a North American church. That is no longer the case. The membership in North America is now around 6 percent of the membership around the world. The American influence and financial support is still strong, but the church in various countries of the world is self-supporting.

The church has become more complex (one might say more bureaucratic). The legal requirements are much more pervasive and numerous, and all this takes time, personnel, and finances.

I served in church employment for nearly 50 years, and I never signed a contract, as far as I can remember. After retirement, when I was asked to continue working at the General Conference, I was requested to sign a contract! Had I become less trustworthy? Of course not. But legal requirements, our litigious society, and the complexity of policies made this written document a requirement.

When I was a young minister in Europe, I always wore, in the pulpit, a black coat with striped trousers, white shirt, and black or silver tie. The ministerial dress in many countries is now much more informal (at times, perhaps, too informal, but I'm no doubt not with it anymore!).

Ministers' wives were generally expected to help their husbands and not be involved in outside employment of their own. This was the case for my parents, and also in my own home. Today the situation has radically changed. Now, with rising costs in the standard of living and the burden of Christian education, it often takes two salaries to live modestly but comfortably.

The whole approach to church life, spirituality, and stewardship has become less legalistic and mathematical, and more relaxed and project-oriented. This change has its good side, but I'm afraid there's also a negative side. Yes, life is more intricate, the demands and pressures come from all sides, and the opportunities and expectations are so abundant that it's easy to be overwhelmed. As a result we can lose our focus, trying to do more and more, and as a consequence do less and less, until we do nothing by thinking about doing everything!

There's always the danger—individually or corporately—to concentrate on strategic, long-range planning, and actually do very little substantial in the present.

Chapter 32

TAKING A STAND

Secular Church Governance

Over the years I've been opposed to secular forms of church governance. A constant danger is the imitation of the American "White House" presidency, or the corporate model, the CEO. Christianity has faced this danger repeatedly for nearly 2,000 years.

Unfortunately, the Christian church has, at times, succumbed to secular temptation and political pressure. Beginning with the second century, churches started to imitate the form of governance of imperial Rome. Soon monarchical bishops became the religious counterparts of Roman governors, and after a couple hundred years the pope assumed much of the titles and trappings of the Roman emperor.

In the United States we have to watch the presidents avoid any psychological temptation to be influenced by the "White House Syndrome," or the CEO temptation. The "buck" stops with the Executive Committee, not with a single person, or kingly power, as Ellen G. White expressed it.

Isolation

I have felt that an isolated or insulated church is not an effective power for evangelism and influence for good in society. The isolated person, pastor, or church soon becomes inward-looking, self-centered, and self-satisfied ("I'm increased in goods and in need of nothing"), increasingly detached from the dynamic realities of life and ineffective. It doesn't help to scratch people or problems where they don't itch. Ignorance is never bliss—it is simply ignorance.

Phonies

I've always disliked anything phony. Much is expected of ministers and church leaders. They are expected to say the right things. The danger is that what they say or do may not be a bona fide reflection of an inner experience with their Lord and work, but simply bogus appearance and outward show. They can go through the motions, say the right, expected, pious things, but where is the spiritual power? There may be a lack of candor and frankness. Individuals can do this so much and for so long that it becomes almost second nature, to the point that they probably don't even realize they have lost their integrity and credibility. To use Dickensian language, they are "artful dodgers." This facade approach to life is phony and falsifies relationships. What makes this pretension so bad and dangerous is that the person who is phony seems unaware of this playacting. I dislike smooth sanctimoniousness.

Conspiracy Seekers

The Seventh-day Adventist Church has, unfortunately, too often attracted to its ranks some individuals who are conspiracy-oriented. They always suspect some intrigue, await some calamity. They not only create rumors but believe every rumor they hear: ministers having affairs; the General Conference infiltrated by Jesuits; an impending national Sunday law; the names of all Adventists specifically recorded in some machine in Brussels, Rome, or elsewhere; church money disappearing like water through a sieve; our schools all gone astray; and the litany goes on, pleasing music to Satan's ears.

Of course, the church is not perfect, because its members are human, and therefore imperfect. I know the Adventist Church and its leaders quite well. There are wonderful, dedicated, and talented people in most leadership posts. I have never detected any significant conspiracy. Individuals, even groups, at times fail, but I've never detected even a hint of a widespread conspiracy at any level where I have been involved.

Jesus warned that at the time of the end there would be "rumors" and false teachers. Our Lord repeated "watch," "be ready," "don't be deceived" by conspiratorial stories.

Racial or Ethnic Prejudice

I grew up in a home in which race or ethnicity was not an issue. All men and women were created equal. I grew up in a country—Switzerland—in which race was not a problem. Of course, in pre-World War II race was not an issue in Switzerland because the country was quite homogenous: everyone was White. There were linguistic and religious divisions, but over a few hundred years the country had found a *modus vivendi* and political/social balance.

After the end of World War II American soldiers came to Switzerland for rest and recreation. The Black soldiers were a great attraction; most Swiss had previously seen Black people only in photographs.

Today, nearly 60 years later, the existential situation in Switzerland is quite different. Out of 7.5 million people, about 25 percent are foreigners, many non-White. Today when something is stolen, a Swiss is likely to say (in the Swiss dialect, of course), "What can you expect, with all these foreigners in the country!"

When I studied at Pacific Union College, race was not a significant topic of discussion for the simple reason there was just a handful of Black students on campus, and they were very popular. Several of them became my colleagues in the mission field and at the General Conference.

The race problem in the United States came to my attention by hitting me between the eyes: I was traveling by train to New York from California and entered a train station in one of the Southern states and discovered there were racially separated restrooms. After 60 years I still remember my shock and surprise. I traveled on, but felt disturbed.

Throughout my public life I always pushed for appointment of people based solely on their talents and capacities. However, with the passing of time it has also become clear to me that an additional criterion has to be taken into consideration: representation. At first this went against my principle of "color blindness" in elections and assigning jobs, but it does make sense in this imperfect "best of possible worlds."

There have been racial tensions in, for example, the British Union Conference. These have been largely worked out; time dispenses patience, patience provides wisdom. I have felt honored during recent years when at two union conference sessions the Black union president—a father figure with balance and sincerity—asked me to come and chair a meeting during which controversial policy matters were to be voted upon. I felt both humbled and honored to be considered, not as a power broker, but as an honest broker.

Search for Titles

One of the traditional weaknesses of ecclesiastics is the desire and at times search for titles and honors. Members of the clergy usually don't get a great deal of money, a symbol of success for the population at large. The age-old temptation for clergy is prestige and influence, and this is often associated with titles and position.

As a child and later a young worker in Europe, I remember the wonderful leveling influence of what we all called each other: "brother" or "sister." This produced a fraternal coequality. The division president was "Brother Olson." As principal of the Italian Union Training School, I was "*Fratello* Beach," and this is what my former Italian students still call me. I love it.

Today titles are growing in importance. Titles are not necessarily bad, but there can be danger that the title becomes more important than the job or calling. The inroads of society are felt. I have always been ill at ease with the use of such titles as "reverend," "right reverend," "very reverend," and "most reverend." The archbishop of York during the Middle Ages became the "primate of England," so the archbishop of Canterbury was called the "primate of all England." The pope in Rome is "his holiness," and therefore, the patriarch of Constantinople is for the Orthodox world "his all holiness." Other ecclesiarchs are called "eminence," "excellency," "beatitude," "venerable," "monsignor," "lord spiritual," etc.

I hope God has a sense of humor, or we'll all be in trouble!

Increasingly, the title bug, which I like to call *morbidus titulus* or *malignant titleitis* is spreading to the Adventist Church. Secretaries of departments want to become directors. Directors want to be called vice presidents; secretaries, executive secretaries; office secretaries, administrative assistants. Fewer and fewer associate directors go by their appointed title, but create a subdepartment within the department so they can be called director. The idea is that it sounds better to be a director of a smaller entity than associate director of the whole! All this can lead to some confusion. Let's not play title games, but be game in doing our work.

Chapter 33

PLACES AND EVENTS WITH SPECIAL MEANING

Driving or walking through where the Berlin Wall once stood, I remember the separations, the fear and even deaths, and complications of passing through such places as Checkpoint Charlie and meeting people "on the other side." Liberty is such a wonderful gift and feeling.

Standing in Bucharest on the balcony of the Parliament speaker's office, at his invitation, I remember him telling me that this was the place President Ceausescu stood and gave speeches, but was booed the last time by the crowd. He then left the building to go to his death, when captured by the insurgents a few hours later. I'm told he was driven by an Adventist chauffeur.

I remember visiting the simple and austere Bethlehem Chapel in Prague. I felt prayerful in the presence and memory of Jan Hus, who preached there, a hero and martyr of the faith, the valiant pre-Reformer, ignominiously burned at the stake during the Council of Constance in 1415.

Visiting under Communism, I remember the home of Dr. and Mrs. Reinhard Schroth in Wittenberg, East Germany. He was a distinguished surgeon, who even authored a surgery manual for medical students, but was held back professionally because he was a Seventh-day Adventist Christian and not a party member. He lived, interestingly, next to the Luther Museum, in what used to be part of the former monastery that was Luther's home after the Reformation in Germany. Here Luther boarded students, who then recorded at meals Luther's "table talks," now preserved in several volumes called in German "Tischreden." While we were eating in the Schroth dining room, Dr. Schroth told me we were sitting where the tower had once stood. He and I remembered, I with a thrill, Luther's famous exclamation: "From this tower I stormed the Papacy!"

Pious Frauds

There are places that lack authenticity and don't ring true: Over the years I have had the opportunity of visiting several places that are supposed to be associated with Jesus or His apostles. Many of these spots are often based on legends and traditions or finds that date at times from many centuries later, and really have no solid, authentic, and verifiable historical foundation. I tend to believe that some bishops or others, with perhaps an eye to the substantial and continuing income that such places generate or receive from pilgrimages, have stated with questionable veracity and missing scholarly support that this is precisely where Jesus was born or walked, was crucified or buried, or where Mary, the mother of Jesus, or an apostle lived or died.

In A.D. 813 the bishop of Santiago de Compostela in Spain claimed that he had discovered the grave of the apostle James! As a result, millions of dollars or other currencies have come in, and continue to do so. When I go to such places, I am not edified by what some churchmen call "pious frauds." Here is a glaring example:

There is a little house inside the Basilica of Loreto in east-central Italy. It is claimed that this is the house in which the mother of Jesus lived in Nazareth. A few centuries ago, the story goes, it was supposedly transported by the angels to a place that is now in Croatia. However, we are told the people there lived evil lives, and the angels arrived again and carried the house to its current location in Loreto, around which the basilica was built. When I asked the monk showing us around whether he actually believed the story, he explained that it was helpful for some people to hear such "faith-strengthening" stories!

A number of authentic places in Israel and Palestine have given me a real and true spiritual lift, such as Gethsemane, the Sea of Galilee, Capernaum, the Mount of Blessings. In Rome the Mamertine Prison looks authentic as a prison in which Paul could have stayed as a prisoner of the emperor, though it is not really certain. Nevertheless, this forbidding place has blessed me the times I dropped down the hole and prayed there. In Athens, Mars Hill is genuine, and I'm inspired by the rocky hill and to stand where Paul faced the intelligentsia of Athens and proclaimed to them the "unknown God" they needed to know and worship.

The great libraries of the world inspire me with awe. I feel so insignificant when I visit the British Museum in London or the Library of Congress in Washington, D.C., or the Bibliotheque Nationale in Paris, or scores of other, smaller but magnificent libraries of accumulated written knowledge. I am, as my name rightly suggests, just a grain of "beach" sand along the ocean of life and the flowing and unending springs of learning. While the concept of eternity is really unfathomable for us as human beings, it does provide the setting to explore the unending galaxies of universal and divine truth, enlightenment, and wisdom.

Chapter 34

RANDOM EXPERIENCES

Honored in Nigeria

I was made an honorary Ibo chief in Aba, Nigeria, in 1980. This ceremony was based on some 20 years of contacts with the church and education work in Nigeria and my involvement in getting east Nigeria to become a conference (from mission status).

I treasure this honor. After more than 30 years I still have my Ibo chief robes, hat, and walking stick. A few years ago I was invited to address a meeting of Nigerian Adventists in California. I took them by surprise when I walked out on the platform with my chief regalia to warm applause.

With the Archbishop of Canterbury

I met Robert Runcie when he was bishop of St. Albans and later archbishop of Canterbury for a decade. He once brought a letter to Eliane for me from Moscow. When I first met him at his residence, he said, "Dr. Beach, I understand you are a bridge builder." One of the titles used by the pope, *Pontifex Maximus*, means "supreme bridge builder." None of us are supreme, but we can, as individuals, be bridge builders. Indeed, with such an army of builders as this, how quickly we could march forward across chasms of separation and over obstacles and prepare people to meet their Lord.

Lambeth Conferences

I attended three Lambeth conferences. Anglican bishops from all over the world meet in Canterbury. Recent sessions have convened every 10 years. The three I attended were 1978, 1988, and 1998 at the University of Kent overlooking the historic city. I was one of about 20 official observers at each conference, presided over by the archbishop of Canterbury.

I went to two garden parties at Buckingham Palace given by Queen Elizabeth II in connection with the conference. (I didn't go in 1988.) I experienced great courtesy and hospitality, but on occasion a little complicated officiousness is found in the Anglican establishment, where everything has to be done "just so."

I met the duke of Edinburgh at the 1998 conference garden party in Buckingham Palace. A few dozen participants among the 800 bishops present were selected to meet either the queen or the royal consort. I was fortunate to be selected to meet the duke of Edinburgh. I wasn't wearing a colorful Episcopal robe, only a Hart, Schaffner, and Marx suit. In trying to read my badge, the duke asked, "What is the Conference of Christian World Communication?"

I answered, "Actually, it's the Conference of Christian World *Communions*."

"I beg your pardon," said His Royal Highness. Then he asked, "Are you a clergyman?"

I said, "Yes, Your Royal Highness."

"Are you ordained?"

Again, "Yes."

The duke then exclaimed, "But not a sign on you, except your Rotary pin!" He knew what it meant, of course, because he was an honorary member of the Rotary Club meeting on Regent Street in London.

And the Door Was Closed

On November 1, 1978, my wife and I were invited by the World Methodist Council to attend the reopening of the remodeled Wesley's Chapel in London, an historical landmark. The queen was to be there with her husband. Parking would be difficult, so Eliane and I decided to go by train from St. Albans, a little more than 20 miles from central London. After looking at the train schedule, we selected a train to get us there in plenty of time before we were to be in our seats at 2:30. However, we didn't realize that the train I had selected didn't run on Sunday! The result was that we arrived at 2:40: too late! We weren't allowed admission, even though the queen arrived a quarter of an hour later. The door was shut! No excuses accepted! We were reminded of the biblical statement "and the door was shut," a valuable spiritual lesson I've never forgotten.

Served by Curiosity

I hoped to get President William Tolbert of Liberia to serve as honorary president of the IRLA: President Tolbert was at that time also president of the Baptist World Alliance. I was in Monrovia for only a couple days, and I couldn't get an appointment. He was a busy man, and his schedule was tight. One of the members of the president's staff suggested that the SDA mission president and I attend a reception in the afternoon at the executive mansion when the new ambassador from Guinea-Bissau would present his credentials.

We sat in the back of the room and were the only White people present, so we sort of stood out. I could see the president on the platform looking at us and wondering who we were. He leaned over to the secretary of state, who leaned over to an aide de camp, who left the platform and came back to us and politely asked who we were. We explained and said we hoped to see the president after the meeting.

After the meeting an official came to me, and to my happy surprise he invited us upstairs where the president would receive us. President Tolbert graciously accepted our invitation to serve as honorary president of the IRLA.

Unfortunately, not long after our meeting, Tolbert was assassinated. Strangely, this happened several times in my life: Indira Gandhi, the archbishop of Uganda, Bishop Samuel of the Coptic Church, and Prime Minister Rajiv Gandhi were all murdered not long after I met them and had pleasant and useful conversations with them.

I can assure everyone that all this had absolutely nothing to do with meeting me! It is sad and sobering, however, to realize that some people you have met and had fruitful meetings with were later killed, essentially for criminal or political reasons.

Friend of the Archbishop

A friend from another world church asked me some 25 years ago, "I know you are a friend of the archbishop of Canterbury. Can you tell me how one becomes friends with such a person?"

I told him, "It's very simple: You become his friend before he becomes the archbishop of Canterbury." This is the easiest way.

Some people, such as Jean Nussbaum, Ernest Steed (my temperance friend and mentor), Gianfranco Rossi, and Neal Wilson, had special gifts in this regard. I learned some pointers from them.

There are elements of luck, foresight, planning, or divine providence when it comes to making significant contacts. I have sometimes missed the boat. I neglected meeting with the cardinal of Kraków (Poland) before he unexpectedly became pope.

I met Martin Luther King, Jr., briefly at a *Pacem in Terris* conference in Geneva, but I didn't realize his full significance, having been in Europe during the civil rights crisis in the United States. I missed the opportunity of really getting acquainted with him and having an in-depth conversation. So I have missed some opportunities.

Witness in the Center of Atheism

In 1986 the official General Conference delegation to Russia was headed by then General Conference president Neal C. Wilson. He truly had a gift for meeting state and religious officials. We received VIP treatment at all airports and were put in the best hotels as guests of church and government. We met with the vice president of the Russian parliament and had a pleasant conversation. I had the unusual opportunity of visiting the Kremlin and saw special rooms not open to visitors at the time, where government diplomatic receptions took place.

One room impressed me in a special way: it was where ambassadors were received and presented their credentials to, at that time, an officially atheistic government. Yet the walls of the chamber were decorated with paintings of biblical themes, beginning with Creation and ending with Christ's glorious appearing! There, in the very heart of an atheistic government, the witness of God's Word was still present!

Now, of course, the situation has changed considerably, and Christianity is acknowledged in Russia, not least in the Kremlin, where the Orthodox Church has a liturgical presence.

First Official Visit to China

In June and July 1994 a General Conference delegation of some 12 people, including several spouses, was able to make its first official visit to China under Communism. While Robert Kloosterhuis, vice president of the GC, headed our group, I was the point man for contacts, since I was acquainted with several of the leaders of the Christian Three-Self Patriotic Movement in China.

The "selfs" are self-governing, self-financing, and self-propagating. In other words, China wanted the church in China to be independent from any foreign control. Adventists have always liked the concept of the "self-supporting church," and the church leadership encourages congregations in all countries to move in that direction, and be self-propagating as much as possible.

Bishop Ting was president of the China Christian Council and principal of the Nanjing Union Theological Seminary. I had met him several times, and had invited him to speak at the 1989 IRLA World Congress in London, which he did. I also knew Rev. Gao Ying, who held several important positions in Chinese churches and in Nanjing Seminary. We had first met in Curitiba, Brazil several years earlier. Humberto Rasi, the director of the GC Education Department, was in our group. Like me, Rasi was vitally interested in getting ministerial training for Adventist ministers in China. The Adventist Church was not allowed to operate its own seminary, but doors were now opened for Adventist students to attend seminaries operated by the Three-Self Movement. This was progress, but not a fully satisfactory solution.

We were treated royally (in harmony with traditional Chinese hospitality), saw some great sites, met inspiring fellow church members, and built some lasting bridges of contact and understanding.

A few years ago our leaders in Hong Kong had difficulty getting an appointment with Bishop Ting, largely because of his advanced age and rather precarious health. I was grateful that he responded to my request, and I was able to go to Nanjing with Robert Wong, a tireless, experienced, and dedicated Chinese leader of the Adventist Church, and reestablish this important link.

Bishop Ting had a perceptive mind and was a persuasive Christian leader and political influence in modern China. I was touched and saddened at our last meeting, when he, sitting in his wheelchair, said twice in a very soft and low voice, "Dr. Beach, how energetic you are."

Organizing World Religious Liberty Congresses

It takes considerable time and effort to organize a successful world religious liberty congress. I must mention that I never had to worry about the finances and logistics of these meetings; I could concentrate on the program and the getting of outstanding speakers, as we did for the Rome and London congresses. While still living in England, I helped PARL get a couple well-known speakers for the Amsterdam conference.

I counted on the expertise of Don Robinson, treasurer of the IRLA, a truly professional and competent congress or session organizer. I also always had the help of Mitchell Tyner, both an ordained minister and practicing lawyer. He has an outstanding legal mind and great business acumen. He has been an invaluable asset to the Seventh-day Adventist Church and many individuals, as well as to PARL and the IRLA in defending, explaining, and promoting religious liberty. Furthermore, he has the rare gift of synthesis, which the pastoral and legal professions seem to have, at times, in short supply!

Chapter 35

TRUST AND TRUE UNITY

Importance in Contacts of Trust and Biblical Unity

I had many contacts with the WCC over nearly half a century. I have known personally the first seven general secretaries of the WCC, beginning with the founding general secretary Willem Visser't Hooft and ending with the last two general secretaries: Samuel Kobia, who was the first African (from Kenya) to serve in this capacity, and the Norwegian Olav Fyske Tveit, with whom I had lunch at the Cosmos Club in Washington, D.C.

Tveit was the first and only WCC general secretary to visit the Seventh-day Adventist world headquarters. He gave me a copy of his installation sermon, in which he affirmed that "the cross is the reality check about all our talk about God and about life." Indeed, the Adventist message is in essence Jesus Christ crucified *and* coming again.

You never know when contacts and friends will make further contacts and friends. I tried to make use of what I've called the "contact ripple effect." I've also consolidated and strengthened my network of friends by staying in contact with them and being at their service and doing favors when opportunities presented themselves. I discovered early on that in interchurch relations or in public affairs, most people are, or feel, so busy with their own affairs that they seldom contact you. So if you want to know how they are doing, or in order to stay informed, you have to contact them!

It is important in interchurch relations that those of another church or religious persuasion be able to trust you and have confidence in you. It isn't as important that they agree with you as it is absolutely necessary that they trust and respect you; that is vital.

I stand up for my church, and can even get somewhat defensive, not to say a little incensed, if my church is attacked. But my integrity, goodwill, and sense of humor usually lead the discussions into quieter and more fruitful outcomes!

My position regarding ecumenism has been quite clearly (some might say "strongly") stated in my book *Ecumenism: Boon or Bane?* (Review and Herald Publishing Association, 1974). From an Adventist viewpoint, ecumenism has its strong points, but also its serious weaknesses. Who can be against the ideal of authentic Christian unity for which Christ prayed? From an Adventist perspective, the problem or issue is not *unity*, but what *kind* of unity. The unity of John 17 is not primarily a oneness in social activism that downplays doctrine, but supremely a oneness of joy, evangelism, truth, sanctification, otherworldliness, and love.

This is the unity we seek.

Chapter 36

A PILGRIMAGE WITH FRIENDS

In my five decades of what could be called a "spiritual pilgrimage," I sought unity of personal fellowship in love, witness, and truth, according to Christ's prayer in John 17 for His followers, and at the same time awaiting the Adventist "world (Greek: *ecumenē*) to come" (see Heb. 2:5). I have met in friendship some wonderful Christian men and women I cannot forget, even in the lengthening corridors of retirement.

Many years ago the British Quaker/Friends leader, Blanche Shaffer, was the first non-Adventist world religious leader to visit me in my St. Albans office. Another outstanding Christian friend is Mary Tanner, full of spiritual vibrancy and theological acumen. She has now been made a dame of the British Empire by England's Queen Elizabeth.

Two archbishops of Canterbury, the late Robert Runcie and George Carey, each represented, with great integrity and refinement, Anglicanism on the world stage. But for me they are simply esteemed friends.

Lord Carey (his title since retirement) told me that his older brother, who had influenced him spiritually, was married to a Finnish Seventh-day Adventist. Her brother is an Adventist pastor in Finland.

Several Catholic leaders have stood out as, some might think, unexpected friends. I refer particularly to Cardinal Walter Kasper, an often smiling and always astute theologian; Archbishop Roland Minnerath of Dijon, a religious liberty expert and advocate; and Bishop Pierre Duprey, late secretary of the Vatican Council for Promoting Christian Unity. He wrote to me, after consulting with various Vatican offices, confirming that the Adventist Sabbath, like the Catholic Sunday, should be a protected right. Monsignor John Radano has been a friend on whom you could count for honesty and correct information. I felt pleased to be asked to write a chapter in the retirement Festschrift prepared in his honor.

Professor Alberto de la Hera is a devout Roman Catholic, but a supporter of Adventist spirituality. He was for several years director of the Religious Affairs Department of Spain's Ministry of Justice. He is a strong advocate of religious liberty, and was helpful to the Adventist Church in Spain in many important ways. I consider him to be one of my dearest friends.

He doesn't speak English too well, and I don't speak much Spanish, so we speak Italian together. He has attended General Conference sessions as a special observer and guest. For many years he was assisted by Professor Rosa Maria Martinez de Codes. She has remained a friend and member of the IRLA's Committee of Experts, and like de la Hera, serves on the IRLA board.

Allen Lee, late general secretary of the World Convention of the Churches of Christ, was a longtime friend, exhibiting desired qualities of a true Christian, as do his successors, Lyndsay and Lorraine Jacobs, now retired in New Zealand. Joe Hale, former general secretary of the World Methodist Council, still exhibits all the qualities of an old friend, and betokens a Christian gentleman par excellence.

My enduring respect for Canon John Peterson of the Washington National Cathedral and former secretary general of the Anglican Consultative Council; and for Mel Robeck, a Pentecostal world figure and seminary professor, is revealed in recommending both to be invited to serve as regular panelists on the nationwide American Religious Town Hall weekly telecast. It feels good to be together again!

The Lutheran World Federation has had some outstanding general secretaries. The first one I knew was the Frenchman André Appel. He was married to an American. He was my predecessor as secretary of the Secretaries of the Christian World Communions. He was followed by Carl Mau, a dear friend, whom I visited, before his relatively early death, in his retirement apartment situated right on Puget Sound. The next Lutheran general secretary was the future bishop of Oslo, Gunnar Stalsett. For several years he served as one of the five individuals who recommend to the Parliament of Norway the yearly Nobel Peace Prize recipient. He has been a friend and has special interest in religious liberty.

His successor was the South African Ishmael Noko. His sister is a Seventh-day Adventist, and both she and her husband teach at Oakwood University in Alabama. Since one of the buildings at Oakwood is named after my father, and Ishmael's wife, Gladys, has the same name as my mother, there is no way that Ishmael and I can avoid being close. Furthermore, we are all "children of Luther"!

A Convinced but Unfulfilled Ecumenist

These memoirs would not be complete without a more substantial reference to Lukas Vischer than what has been mentioned briefly elsewhere in this book.

For many years he was the guiding theologian, not only of the Commission on Faith and Order, but of the WCC in general. He opened for me—for good or ill—the significance and aims of the ecumenical movement. He was so convinced of its inevitable success and of the onward march of organized unity that I think he believed the Seventh-day Adventist Church would in due course join the WCC. Although I made it quite clear in all our contacts that this was not going to happen, he probably believed that surely I would see the light!

Looking back over the past several decades of my meaningful association with this dedicated Christian, I believe that in some ways he ultimately became a disappointed figure. For some years it looked like he might well become the next WCC general secretary. Then he seemed to run into opposition from sectors within the WCC, including some Orthodox leaders. The general secretary at that time, Philip Potter, decided to invoke an unevenly applied WCC rule—namely that executives had to vacate their position after nine years. Since Vischer had already served several years beyond the nine, he was forced to quit.

I have always felt that his dismissal deprived the WCC of a respected and viable candidate for general secretary. Vischer went on to serve for several more years as the ecumenical secretary for the Swiss Council of Churches and professor at the University of Bern, though continuing to live in Geneva. However, some of the sparkle appeared to have vanished from his personality. Moreover, his departure seemed to coincide with a substantial decline of the WCC in size of staff, financial resources, and influence.

It is my sense that a dedicated and gifted theologian and leader had been sidetracked or put aside and perhaps even became an unfulfilled man. I must pay tribute to Vischer's keen mind and recognize his decisive help in getting the Seventh-day Adventist Church recognized in the late 1960s as a Christian world communion.

Though in recent years I had little contact with Vischer, when he died in 2010 I felt that I had lost an old and lamented friend, and the WCC a notable figure, such as one finds hard to discover in current ecumenical ranks.

Blessed Communion

The four general secretaries of the World Communion of Reformed Churches (formerly World Alliance of Reformed Churches) have been esteemed friends. Marcel Pradervand, as chair of the meeting in the fall of 1968, welcomed me as a participant in the gathering of Secretaries of Christian World Communions. For the first time, the General Conference of Seventh-day Adventists was recognized as a Christian world communion. This was quite a change that we were able to work out, in glaring contrast to the word "sect," which was indiscriminately used in many places, high and low; often, at times, with even more pejorative terminology. This was the beginning of a major shift or change in how the Seventh-day Adventist Church was perceived; informed respect was growing.

Coming back to the WCRC: Edmond Perret, a Swiss like Pradervand, was the next general secretary. He and I became warm friends. When he retired, Milan Opocensky, a fine Czech theologian took over. I had first met him in Prague several years earlier in connection with meetings of the Christian Peace Conference. We became friends. Unfortunately, he died quite unexpectedly, soon after his retirement.

The current general secretary of the WCRC is the Ghanaian Setri Nyomi. He presided at my retirement dinner, with all the speech trappings and food trimmings, thanking me for my long service as Secretary of the Conference of Christian World Communions. This event took place in Nicosia, Cyprus, in 2003. After 32 years (I suppose a sort of "ecumenical" record) I felt the time had come. I must confess that rationally I knew I was doing the right thing, but psychologically it was not easy, because so much of my life had been tied to the development and nurture of the Christian World Communions. I felt as if I was losing part of my life. In a way this turned out to be true.

Changing of the Guard

However, my successor in Washington, D.C., at the General Conference of Seventh-day Adventists was ready to take over, and John Graz has done a splendid job. He is well organized, and everybody likes him. Things run like a fine Swiss watch, honoring his nationality. This makes me very proud and happy. I feel like telling him, "Your servant can now go in peace."

I thank God He has allowed me to discover and know all these and other friends, brothers, and sisters in Christ. I just had to cross the bridges we were building and find them and become their friend, because they were always there, ready to be friends.

Chapter 37

TRAVEL AND OTHER REFLECTIONS

One of the interesting aspects of my overseas and General Conference service has been travel. Despite the saying that "travel broadens your feet," travel greatly expands the mind, though, of course, it can be tiring and difficult at times. Travel is certainly more comfortable now than in the days of the pioneers. Speed is great, yet it was more relaxing to travel across the Atlantic by ship for five or more days than flying to Europe, eastern Asia, or elsewhere all night and plunging into appointments as soon as you arrive.

One thing about the great Adventist family is that church leaders visiting various countries and churches are normally well received and often treated royally. M. V. Campbell, a General Conference general vice president, told me more than 40 years ago: "Remember, Bert, when people come to meet you at the airport and take you to your hotel, appointments, and meals, it isn't because of you, it's because of your position."

Well, 40 years later I'm "decreasing" (to use biblical language) so that others can increase. But I'm still usually warmly received and treated, though retired. Maybe it's because I've become a kind of father figure, or maybe it's because I have so many friends, or perhaps, just maybe, the vice president was only partly right: We Adventists are *family*.

All Are Yours

The apostle Paul, in writing to the church in Corinth, pointed out that "all things are yours" (1 Cor. 3:21, NIV). What a wealth of culture, civilization, history, art, knowledge, language, natural beauty, human warmth, and friendship has been at my disposal in all those many lands—140 at last count—all these years. What a gift! What enrichment! Yes, all are mine. Paul adds that we must, however, remember that we "are Christ's, and Christ is God's." That's the framework, even in travel.

I have had the privilege of seeing many, probably most, of the cultural, heritage, and scenic wonders of the world. I treasure these marvelous gifts.

Being a trained historian, I suppose, has doubly enriched this gift.

Yet some don't appreciate such riches. Years ago the mother of one of my college associates at Pacific Union College was visiting Florence, Italy, and I showed her the riches of Renaissance Florence, including the original marble statue *David*, by Michelangelo. In answer to my comment "Isn't it marvelous," she answered, "Yes, but the one we have at Forest Lawn Cemetery (a plaster cast reproduction) is better."

On another occasion in Germany, a member of our travel group stayed in his car while in Worms, not interested in walking a few yards to see the place identified by a plaque where Martin Luther had stood in 1521 to challenge the emperor and the pope in favor of God's truth and the burgeoning Reformation!

Early Friends

The friends we make early in life often tend to leave a permanent imprint. There is something special in childhood and college friendships that give them a lasting quality. Class reunions have more than symbolic meaning. From time to time I still go to Bern for reunions with my old classmates, although the ranks are thinning out and the few of us who remain are beginning to feel like "the last of the Mohicans."

Hans (Hai) Beat Herzog was in my class at the Freies Gymnasium. Hai lived just a couple hundred yards from my home. We became close friends, and as a result, he and his mother joined the Seventh-day Adventist Church. He married Anny, one of the three Tissot sisters with whom my sisters and I grew up in the Bern church. I was at both their wedding and their golden wedding anniversary celebration.

Hai later became a dentist in Olten, honoring tradition by following in the footsteps of his father, grandfather, and great-grandfather, who had all been dentists! Hai became the elder and financial pillar of the Adventist Church in Olten, and Anny served as treasurer for more than 50 years. Anny used to say with humor that they had a "prophet's room" in their home, where I often stayed.

Anny and Hai both died recently, and this has been an irreplaceable earthly loss for me. They have one son, Hans Jörg, a senior airline pilot, and we keep in touch. He and his companion, Myrta, asked me to conduct a private prayer service on the little hill connected to their "Chalet Topaz" in Grindelwald. We gently scattered the ashes of Hai and Anny on the lush green meadow facing the famous Eiger alpine mountain peak and the nearby glacier. "When the saints go marching in, Lord, I want to be in that number," with Hai and Anny, "when the saints go marching in."

Children and the Church

I know my parents received great satisfaction in seeing all three of their children involved in the Adventist Church and married to church members. My wife and I have had a similar lasting joy. When your children follow you in the same spiritual footsteps, it makes you feel that your imperfect example did not drive them away. Our two children went to Adventist schools, and the combined influence of home, school, and church has provided a gratifying result. It is a grand-slam experience! I'm proud of our daughters, Danielle and Michele. I pay tribute to Eliane's strong, loving, and stable influence, especially with an often-absent husband.

I have, over the years, met so many parents who suffer and are greatly disappointed because one or more of their children have drifted away from the church, and they feel the family no longer presents an "unbroken circle." Our prayers have been answered, and now we pray for our four grandchildren, Philippe, Adriane, Emma, and Alyssa, who live in an even more difficult, demanding, and dangerous world.

Hardly an Extended Family

My parents, two sisters, and I formed a warm, cohesive, but somewhat isolated family. I never fully experienced the boon of an extended family. My parents were missionaries in Europe when I was born, and we lived several thousand miles across the Atlantic from our nearest relatives. The missionary term to Europe was 10 years before a furlough was granted. No relative was able to come and visit us in Europe. I was 8 years old before my parents had their first furlough in 1936. I then saw all my grandparents, aunts, uncles, and cousins for the first time, and, in some cases, for the only time, because the next furlough was again 10 years away.

World War II broke out in 1939, and we were increasingly cut off, with very little and often belated news reaching us. Before we returned to the United States again in 1946 at the end of the war, my father's mother had died. I have few but very warm memories of this wonderful Irish woman. My father's only brother, Jim, had died (he and his wife were so nice to me); one of my mother's sisters had died (such a nice and loving person). These were all people I liked but did not have the opportunity to know very well. My youngest and favorite uncle, Bryan, was killed while serving as a pilot in the U.S. Air Force. In fact, we heard about his death several months after it happened. On two occasions I was able to visit his grave in the well-maintained American military cemetery outside Cambridge, England.

I saw very little of these good people, but I felt blessed the few times I did see them. My father's parents were pillars of the Adventist Church in Idaho. Grandfather Herbert was a longtime member of the Idaho Conference executive committee. My mother's parents were Southern Baptists, but proud of their Adventist preacher grandson. My grandfather Artemus Corley was a pillar of honesty and rather outspoken, even a little eccentric. But most of the town of Haskell, Texas, came out for his funeral.

He sort of embarrassed me many decades ago one Sunday at the Baptist church in Haskell. Toward the close of the service he got up and complained before the whole congregation that I hadn't been invited to speak or pray! As a result, I was swiftly asked to offer the benediction! On another occasion my grandfather Corley told his local church he wanted to put up a representation of the Ten Commandments in the church they were building. When the board demurred, he said he wouldn't give anything to the new building! When I got a little too outspoken, my mother would say that I got that from my grandfather.

Price of Mission Service

Eliane and I have never had a grandparent, aunt, uncle, or first cousin from my side of the family visit our home. This is the price we paid for mission service and living in Europe for so many years. We lived a few thousand miles away, and most of my relatives lived a countrified life, were not world travelers, and were quite happy to stay in their home states.

My uncle Bob Corley could have visited us while we were living in England. However, he had served in the United States Navy in the Pacific during World War II. He said, "Bert, during the war I promised the good Lord that if He brought me safely home, I'd never leave the U.S. again." He kept his promise.

I'm sorry for this. We love our relatives and do keep in contact by phone with several cousins. Fortunately, several of my wife's relatives from Belgium have visited us. I'm always warmly received by our relatives in Idaho, Texas, California, Michigan, Belgium, France, and Switzerland.

Living in Two Worlds

Though I've never been accused of having a "split personality," there's little doubt I have lived in two worlds. I'm not referring to the two worlds in which every dedicated Christian must live: the spiritual world of God's kingdom and the secular world. I'm referring to the two geographical and cultural worlds in which my life has been almost equally divided by time.

People often ask whether I'm American or European. Culturally and linguistically I'm quite European; I can very well pass as Swiss or French.

My father used to say that I often thought like a Bernese, and the use of my arms and hands in public speaking remind me of my years in France and Italy.

I esteem my European background and education and love the five European countries in which I lived. I still follow the ups and downs of some of my favorite soccer teams and tennis greats.

But I'm also a patriotic American, whose feelings for my country have been formed by 45 years of separation. I love the United States as a country of freedom, justice, independence, and generosity; I love it as the "land of the free and home of the brave." This has made me more sensitive in religious liberty work to any sinister encroachments on civil and religious freedom that risk turning the "lamblike" nation of fairness into an arrogant, apocalyptic old "dragon."

I have lived in Paris. What a great city and history. I have lived in Bern, Switzerland, the city of my roots. That's where I grew up. The local dialect is my language. I visit this city with nostalgia. I've lived in Florence, Italy. What a marvelous city of art and so many warm and wonderful people. I've lived in England, mostly in St. Albans. That's where my "public life" began. We go back there whenever we can, see the Roman ruins, the splendid cathedral-abbey, and walk down memory's path. We love Devon, Cornwall, Wales, and many other places. Watford is where our daughter, Michele was born. I've lived in Brussels, the city of my wife, Eliane, where we were married more than 58 years ago, where our eldest daughter Danielle, was born. We even lived for a few months in Bouaké, Cote d'Ivoir, a valuable learning experience. That's where Michele caught malaria, but it manifested itself only six months later back in England. I've loved living in every one of these places.

Where would I go back and live? I've learned one thing from life: you really can't go back and live again where you've lived before. Life moves on and things change; people move and die. I have great and enduring memories that buoy me up when things get a little difficult at times. But I don't want to go back. I must move forward. The "greatest place" is where I live *now*—the Washington, D.C., area.

Chapter 38

MONEY AND POSSESSIONS

Until late in life I never had much money. Neither did my parents or ancestors going back 10 generations when ye pilgrim John Beach arrived in Connecticut from England in 1639 (or very soon thereafter) with lots of courage, few possessions, and a work ethic that helped found New Haven and Wallingford. My ancestors were usually the youngest born in the family, who normally moved on to start a new life and living, because in those years the eldest son inherited most of the father's business and possessions.

When I accepted the call to Italy in 1952 to serve as principal of the Italian Union Training School, I never inquired what my salary would be. It was $100 a month (60,000 lira, to be precise), which was about a third of what I had received in California as principal of the West Liberty Union School.

When I married in 1954, I got a salary increase of $10 per month. I jokingly told Eliane that this was what she was expected to live on. We enjoyed living in Italy; we never felt deprived.

However, as far as I know, all my ancestors had useful and fulfilled lives. I think they understood that material possessions in themselves do not make the "good life." For happiness and success, you have to reach out first "above yourself" in the vertical, God-ward dimension, then "beyond yourself" in the horizontal human-ward dimension. This is what makes life worth living, for true success is not measured simply in dollars, diplomas, or material possessions, but by hitching your wagon to a great cause.

Having come into possession of some funds through inheritance, Eliane and I have been happy to endow three Adventist schools each with a yearly lectureship: Newbold College in England, Saleve Adventist University in France, and Italian Adventist College Villa Aurora in Florence, Italy. Members of the Beach family have, for more than three generations, been associated with these important institutions in Europe, either on the board, as faculty, or as students. These lectureships aim at highlighting in an academic/scholarly setting aspects of the Adventist Church's global mission, and religious liberty.

Several relatives and friends have given support. My nephew, David Beach Cotton, and his wife, Shery, have given substantial financial help. After a distinguished career in academic medicine, David is currently the CEO of several large and growing health maintenance organizations in Michigan and other states.

Chapter 39

WHAT A UNIVERSE! WHAT A GOD! WHAT LESSONS!

While serving the Seventh-day Adventist Church in various capacities for some 60 years, I've discerned from the Giver of life a few important lessons about life. I learned from family, friends, and coworkers; from my successes and accomplishments; but even more, I admit, from my deficiencies and insufficiencies. Here I'm not featuring obvious and important factors, such as the centrality of Christ, hard work and dedication, the preciousness of health, the increasing value of passing time, and not living in isolation, etc.

As a child I felt that God was a wonderful being, as revealed by Jesus Christ. As I got older, I began to understand—only very partially—the greatness of the loving Creator, not only of this galaxy, but of billions of others as well. God's laws are a magnificent serendipity, a gracious gift from an all-powerful God. Think of it: a change of as little as 0.5 percent of the strength of the nuclear force, or 4 percent of electric force, would destroy either nearly all carbon or all oxygen in the stars and, presumably, life as we know it. If the mass of the sun were 20 percent more or less, we would have temperatures hotter than Mars or colder than Venus! (Stephen Hawking, *The Grand Design*, pp. 152, 159, 160). Our universe and its laws have an awesome precision that is tailor-made, thus requiring a divine Tailor to support our universe and every moment of our existence, with no room for trial or error, alteration of any dimension, or fine-tuning on the way. So for me, the inherent edification of life is what a wonderful world God has provided for us, though marred temporarily by sin!

This vast universe of time and space offers all of us an unending and challenging object lesson of eternal study and never-ending praise by the redeemed. This is foundational for my belief and outlook on life.

Found Is Better

Being lost is always an unpleasant experience, especially if you are a child, but even more for the parents! I was about 5 years old when I used to go with my mother to an open-air market at Place d'Italie, a short distance from where we lived in Paris, where she would buy fresh vegetables and fruit. I remember that on one occasion we became separated. One of the good vendors who operated a stall stood me on a chair or table so that I could be easily seen, though I was not for sale, and gave me something to chew on! In due course, my mother found me, to the great relief of both of us.

My daughter Danielle had a "gift" for wandering off and getting lost in crowds from time to time. Our worst experience was on the boardwalk in Atlantic City at the North American Youth Congress in 1960. We were with friends, Aldo and Paule Vacca, and their two children, Bruno and Francoise. Aldo had been with me on the staff at the school in Florence. He had studied medicine in Italy, but decided to immigrate to the United States. We continued our friendship while I taught at Columbia Union College (now Washington Adventist University), and he launched a successful medical practice nearby in Wheaton, Maryland. His wife, Paule Lavanchy, was the daughter of a longtime church leader in France and Belgium.

Somehow, Danielle and Bruno wandered off and then got separated from each other. The word "kidnapping" had recently become part of the American vocabulary. We were almost in a panic. To cut the story short, they were both found by the police, and all ended well.

There was, however, a tragic sequel. Soon afterward, Eliane and I went to Europe to live in England. Perhaps three years later the Vaccas went on a ski trip with their two children, and during the drive their car was hit by a truck at a crossroads. They were all killed, and the family we knew had been wiped out!

However, after we had returned to Europe, Aldo and Paule had had twins. They were too young to go skiing, so they had stayed home with friends and thus escaped the catastrophe. What was to happen to the remaining children? They had no relatives in the United States. My father, then secretary of the General Conference, stepped in and helped make court-approved legal and financial arrangements for their future. Jean Lavanchy, Paule's brother, a minister in France, and his wife, Jaqueline, agreed to raise the twins as their own children. Later Jean became president of the Franco-Belgian Union, as his father and my father had been. Unfortunately, he died unexpectedly from a heart attack at one of the Paris railway stations, still a couple of years from retirement.

I mention these experiences because they illustrate in our day the wonderful "lost" stories or parables that Jesus used so beautifully to highlight the Father's abiding love for His lost children, and the assurance that there is always a place waiting for the "lost and found" in the mansions of our heavenly home.

Seven Realities

Some other aspects of one's life experience are not often mentioned because they are, perhaps, not so obvious. But they seem significant to me.

1. Sincerity and honesty are not enough. Early in my career I tended to believe that what counted, at all cost, was simply the truth, revealed in honesty and sincerity. Let the chips fall where they may.

I remember two cases during which this philosophy dominated my actions. I was sitting on a union committee discussing the hiring of new ministerial interns. There was in that country a requirement that to be taken into the Adventist ministry a candidate should have canvassed (sold church literature) during the school's summer holidays. One candidate had not done so. His father, a member of the union committee, was, presumably, anxious to see his son follow in his ministerial footsteps.

When the canvassing issue was raised, he said: "I don't understand why we have this rule requiring young ministerial candidates to have canvassed."

I immediately jumped into the discussion on the side of "absolute truth": "How can you say this, when you have been the leading advocate of this policy? Suddenly you now want to change it?" The result was that the father started weeping, and I realized I'd spoken unkindly.

A few years later I sat on a division committee, and one of the members said something and argued a point that was simply wrong. I "told him off" in a rather direct and no-nonsense way and tone.

He complained later that I had "undressed him in public."

In both cases I feel I was "right," but still "dead wrong." Why? Because I overlooked the great Christian principle that sincerity and honesty need to be balanced and tempered by kindness and empathy. Sincerity at its best must be informed by understanding.

The letter of honesty can kill, but the spirit of kindness and generosity "maketh alive." I'm grateful that in both cases the men involved remained my friends.

2. You cannot go back to your former life. The Salle Blumenthal was the large hall at the Sorbonne where I presented my oral doctoral dissertation defense in May 1958. When I returned to Paris with my wife, Eliane, some 40 years later, I wanted to show her around. We entered the university, and I asked one of the guards, a campus porter/receptionist called a *huissier* in French, where we could find the Salle Blumenthal. I was told there was no such hall! I insisted the room had existed in 1958.

Disappointed, I showed Eliane a few places, such as the library, the History Department, and the statue of Robert de Sorbon, founder of the College de Sorbonne in 1257.

Later, when exiting, the official stopped me and said that he had looked into the matter, and that I was right, there had been such a hall, but recent restructuring had eliminated it! You cannot go back to previous places in life. Life is not static; it rolls on. Friends move away or die, circumstances change, often radically. You can't go back to the imagined "good old days of yesteryear." We have to move forward, grow, and develop.

This is even more important in the third millennium, because thinking, standards, jobs—just about everything—is in a constant state of flux. If we don't expand in strength and stand firmly both intellectually and spiritually, the rolling sociological and ideological tide will either submerge us, drown us, or sweep over us and leave us behind, out of date, and out of touch, a dry human anachronism.

3. *Humor is the elixir of life.* It is the fluid or sweetener that helps make the difficulties of daily existence go down. Of course, humor is not a panacea, nor, as many in medieval times looked for, a magic potion that could prolong life indefinitely. It is never a remedy for sin, which needs a loving and forgiving Savior. It does, however, function as a shield against the knocks and absurdities of human existence.

Seeing the comical side of people and events provides a glimmer of light in darkness and vigor in occasions of trial or lassitude. Adventists with long, pessimistic "horse faces" risk being a contradiction in terms.

4. *God is not mocked.* When dealing with injustices in and outside of the church, with individuals who seemingly get by scot-free, I remember the saying my mother told me at various times during my childhood in Bern: "The mills of the gods grind slowly, but they grind exceedingly small."

I witnessed this process on various occasions. You and I may be mocked, but God is not mocked: "For whatsoever a man soweth, that shall he also reap" (Gal. 6:7). We see this again and again. Looking back over my long service in church leadership, I have few regrets. My beloved church treated me exceedingly well, and my coworkers have been great people to work with. There was one time that I had felt that an injustice had been committed, and some short-term embarrassment was caused. But within a few brief years the four people involved had lost their positions, probably to their shock and, no doubt, discomfiture. The Lord of the church is not an absentee landlord. He is merciful and forgiving; He is also just. He takes the right time His wonders to perform.

5. *Life is not simple, but complex and complicated.* One of the lessons

I've learned is that life is not as simplistic and neat as I imagined when I was much younger. It is considerably more convoluted, problematic, colorful, and *nuancée,* as the French would say.

We like to see things simply in terms of right or wrong, black or white, but life is more messy and entangled. There are many gray areas and other colors. Satan, the master painter of deception, likes to use a palette with many hybrid colors, some sparkling, but he also uses lots of grays that appear dull and dreary and seemingly undetermined and ambiguous. In this way he can, and does, confuse the majority of people. We all need to be aware of this method of temptation and be watchful.

When I was a college student, I thought Uriah Smith's book *Thoughts on Daniel and the Revelation* was an almost infallible presentation of biblical prophecy. Now I realize that he provided an exciting panorama of church history and shed great light on those two biblical books, but he is not the final word on Daniel and Revelation. We now have additional light and discernment provided by sound Adventist scholarship and ongoing history. We'll be blessed by an even more complete comprehension that awaits us, the result of the divine gift arising from serious Bible study.

Biblical prophecy is a great source of illumination down life's road, but should never be superficially interpreted by simplistic and short-lived newspaper headlines, or brief and selective use of sources.

6. Success in life requires concentration. This is another of life's lessons I've had to learn. Like most people, I have at times suffered from attention deficiency, not in a morbid sense, but sufficient enough to slow my progress toward reaching the goal. This was brought vividly to my mind in September 2011, during a trip to Alaska.

I met Libby Riddles, Alaska's folk hero for being the first woman to win the Iditarod dog-team sled race. In her book *Race Across Alaska* she wrote: "Nothing else existed in the world, just the team and me in this sea of a storm. When my mind could wander for just an instant, it didn't go far. From concentrating completely on finding the next marker, I went to arctic survival. . . . Danger existed just a few feet on either side of the trail, a few feet from those precious markers, and my senses were on alert" (p. 182).

What inspiring words! We are all in the race of life, faced with "sin survival." The salvation pathway is narrow, with danger lurking on both the liberal and conservative sides of life's path. Concentration on Christ and the truth markers is the prescription.

I remember Paul's great statement: "But one thing I do: . . . straining toward what is ahead, I press on toward the goal to win the prize for which God has called me heavenward in Christ Jesus" (Phil. 3:13, 14, NIV).

7. We need long-range mission and vision. My father, Walter Beach, used to counsel, "Don't major in minors." I agree, and advise not to concentrate on the unending multitude of individual trees that can distract and confuse. We need to look at the forest of life, and keep before us and follow with integrity the revealed tableau of worldwide mission. Decisiveness is important in leadership. That may explain why academics can be weak in leadership while being strong in analysis. They often lack directness, and yes, a certain boldness, and may also suffer from what is often called "analysis paralysis," because they see all the different colors and hues of problems that can obscure the total picture.

It's possible for church administration to deal largely with today or the few months or years until the next election. Our process of reasoning must not keep us in the labyrinth of immediate confusion or achieving small gains by moving in various directions. I tried, as best I could, to think in terms of both the long-range judgment of history and God's judgment of eternity.

Chapter 40

THE REVIVED SPIRITUAL LIFE

A few years ago I attended a meeting of U.S. church leaders. A key theme of the conference dealt with nurturing one's spiritual life while involved in the multitudinous administrative tasks requiring one's attention. After more than 40 years of meeting with church leaders from many diverse geographic, denominational, and theological backgrounds, I've come to view three different classes of people in church leadership: (1) traveling bureaucrats, (2) status and title monuments, and (3) men and women of God. It is a privilege to associate with and be blessed by these many leaders, particularly in the last category.

It isn't easy to write about my own spiritual life. Although by nature friendly, outgoing, and probably, at times, too outspoken, I'm also rather private when it comes to my spiritual life and my relationship to God. Spiritual counselors or facilitators in group dynamics ask us, at times, to be vulnerable vis-à-vis other people. I don't like being "vulnerable" and holding hands in group sessions.

Nevertheless, let me try to say a few things that seem meaningful to this longtime and imperfect church leader.

My personal definition of true spirituality is brief and unpretentious: It's being in harmony with God's will. This is my daily desire. I ask God, "Teach me thy way, O Lord, and lead me in a plain path" (Ps. 27:11). There's no need here for considerable theological complexity and sophistication.

My church is a Bible and Christ-centered church. However, it may surprise some to hear that I endeavor to guide my public life by asking myself four questions of seemingly secular origin, but which I believe have a Christian foundation: 1. Is it the truth? 2. Is it fair to all concerned? 3. Will it build goodwill and better friendships? 4. Will it be beneficial to all concerned?

This is the Four-Way Test of Rotary International. I find these questions helpful and down-to-earth in sustaining and guiding an ethical/spiritual/administrative life.

The Revived Spiritual Life

Adventist spirituality is usually less organized than it seems to be in some other communions. We don't follow spiritual exercise books, breviaries, or canonical hours. We don't set daily or seasonal prayers, or have appointed spiritual advisors. While such structured approaches may prove helpful to some, there is a great risk of formalism. Praying mechanically by rote does not nourish a spiritual relationship with God. On the other hand, our usually more relaxed, extemporaneous approach may lack focus and be less targeted.

Adventist spirituality, including my own, is also less contemplative or mystic, and more pragmatic and "action" oriented, thus aiming at authenticity by revealing the *fruit* of the spirit. While there may be no ecstasy, neither should we be lost in constant busyness. The life in Christ includes restfulness because there's abiding, peaceful trust. In this connection, retirement has its advantages.

Like other Christians who believe in and emphasize creation, I receive a spiritual uplift by being surrounded by the wonders of nature; especially the starry heavens at night when there are no artificial lights to interfere. Camping out at night in high-altitude Ethiopia without a human light in sight provided an unforgettably starry spectacle. The incomprehensible and awesome vastness of the expanding universe puts me in my place. Yet this almighty creator God loves and looks after each of us, and I can call Him intimately, "Abba, Father."

Like most preachers, I receive spiritual nourishment while preparing sermons and in writing articles. I have a strong suspicion that in this ministry, my soul is more nourished than those who have to listen, or per chance, read!

Two little books have been helpful to me. One is *Ds Nöie Teschtamänt Bärndütsch*. This is the New Testament in the Swiss-Bernese dialect. There is a nitty-gritty power in this version. Since this language is usually unwritten, it is easier to read by talking it silently (or audibly) to yourself. It's so down-to-earth, in some ways the opposite of the glorious majesty of the King James Version. I like to read it before going to sleep. I'm grateful to my old Adventist friend, Henri Kempf, pioneer missionary to Burkina Faso and Togo, with his wife, Hilda, for giving this New Testament to me. Their own Alsatian dialect is quite close to Bernese.

Then there is that essence of Seventh-day Adventist spirituality, the small book *Steps to Christ*, by Ellen G. White. Written more than a century ago, it is simple, demanding, but encouraging. I have distilled for my personal edification some two dozen points or steps that are helpful in teaching about and nourishing spiritual life. Here are just a few of those rallying points that can revive, energize, and revitalize the spiritual vitality of church leaders and members.

1. *You don't have to fear God, yet much of religion is built on the fear of God.* He loves us with an everlasting love. Satan wants us to feel hopelessly estranged from a God who is often characterized as a severe judge, a rigid and demanding accountant and time-keeper, or an exacting creditor.

2. *God's love is revealed also in suffering and difficulties that result from sin.* The trials of life—the thorns and thistles that emerged after the fall and prick us—are appointed for our training and uplifting.

3. *Education, culture, willpower, all have their place, but "they cannot purify the springs of life" (p. 18).* In themselves they lead to the dead end of salvation by works. Christ is the power that gives us victory; His grace alone can quicken our lifeless faculties. He is the only medium of spiritual communication between God and human beings (p. 20).

4. *Regarding repentance, an important thought is often overlooked: "Repentance includes sorrow for sin, and a turning away from it."* I need to lament sin, rather than sin's unpleasant consequences (p. 23). David understood this. That's why, despite his shocking sins, God could call David a man after His own heart.

5. *The sins that are especially offensive to God are not so much the visible outward acts that we so readily highlight and condemn, but internal pride, selfishness, and covetousness, for they are contrary to the very essence and "benevolence of His character" (p. 30).*

6. *God's authority is not based on, nor requires, blind submission, but rather it freely appeals to our intellect and conscience.* Here is a fundamental religious liberty principle: God cannot accept an homage that is not willingly and intelligently given. How many atrocious and foolish crimes have been committed by so-called Christians who try to force others to worship God in certain ways?

God gives us a wonderful gift—the power of choice—and we can yield our will to Christ and ally ourselves with the power that is above all powers (p. 48).

7. *Our character is revealed "not by occasional good deeds and occasional misdeeds, but by the tendency of the habitual words and acts" (p. 58).* Nothing haphazard here.

8. *E. G. White gave two simple yet dynamic definitions regarding prayer and its vitality.* She wrote that prayer is "the opening of the heart to God as to a friend" and is our "key in the hand of faith to unlock heaven's storehouse" of spiritual nourishment (pp. 93, 94, 95). Our Friend controls an inexhaustible and boundless "storehouse" the size of swirling galaxies.

9. Some individuals mistakenly see the pinnacle of spirituality in quiet and permanent retreat-like separation from the world. God does not expect His disciples to retire from society, their fellow human beings, and the world's responsibilities. He expects Christian leaders to live like Christ, between the mountain and the multitude. A retreat can be spiritually invigorating, but we have to be socially active and involved in meaningful, down-to-earth activity for God and His church. Otherwise we can easily lose focus, and our prayers become formal, routine, and selfishly detached from the dynamic realities of life situations (p. 101). We need the challenging and sanctifying influence of others—colleagues, friends, spouse, children, and yes, grandchildren, not least my own!

10. Jesus said we should be of "good cheer," for He has overcome the world. We need the nourishment provided by a positive attitude to achieve consistent growth in spiritual stature. Joy and gladness drive spiritual development. A "horse-face" Christian is a contradiction in terms. Gloom and moroseness starve and crush the spirit. We need a sanctified sense of humor.

I don't need extraordinary abilities or great occasions to work for God, and neither does anyone else. Together we need to go forward by faith, step by step, quietly and humbly creating ripples that the Spirit will swell into waves of divine blessing. We don't have to weary ourselves with anxiety about success. Spirituality does not "quench the light of joy" (p. 121). Christ discerned in every human being infinite growth potential.

Today we are still imperfect. But the redeemed will stand "without fault before the great white throne" (p. 126), every imperfection having been removed by the blood of Christ. The joyous glory of Christ's character is imparted through divine grace. Here at the end of my life the words of the incomparable hymn writer Isaac Watts summarize the challenge of God's love and my response in nourishing spirituality, revival, and union with Christ:

"Were the whole realm of nature mine,
   That were a tribute far too small;
   Love so amazing, so divine,
   Demands my life, my soul, my all."

APPENDIX

HONORS AND DISTINCTIONS

Over the years, especially when getting older and heading into and through retirement, I received recognition and awards from inside and outside the Adventist Church. They still trickle in! While these are, naturally, appreciated, they do humble you when you realize how many servants of the church go quietly about their work, often unrecognized, and are more deserving. Here are, with some hesitation, as a sort of epilogue, a few of the honors I've received. They are mentioned only for historical purposes:

Non-Adventist Honors
Honorary Ibo chief in Aba, Imo State, Nigeria (1980)
Key to the city of Yokohama, Japan (1982)
Secretary of the Conference of Secretaries of Christian World Communions for 32 years, receiving a small trophy at a recognition dinner in Nicosia, Cyprus, in 2003 and a plaque in Buenos Aires in 2004
Several honors were received in Poland, because of the special relationship of more than 40 years: the Order of Bishop Horuda from the Polish National Church; the Order of St. Magdalene from the Polish Orthodox Church (twice: first bronze and then silver); honorary member

of the Polish Bible Society (three others have been so honored, including Billy Graham). Honorary Th.D. from the Warsaw Protestant/Orthodox Theological Faculty (Academy) in 1987. A "knighthood" from the president of Poland: the Knight's Cross of the Order of Merit of the Polish Republic (1998)

American of the Year award from the American Religious Town Hall Meeting (2005)

Award of Merit as secretary-general emeritus of the International Religious Liberty Association (1997)

Human Rights Leadership Award from *Freedom Magazine* (1997)

A half-dozen medals from various Christian churches

Included for more than 20 years in *Who's Who in America* (Marquis)

Included in the *World Christian Encyclopedia's* Who's Who of World Christian Church Leaders as one of 490 people listed for the 1970s and 1980s (1982)

Appointed chairman emeritus of the John H. Weidner Foundation (2005)

Awards and Honors From the Seventh-day Adventist Church
Alumnus of the Year, Pacific Union College (1997)

President's Leadership Award, Andrews University (1998)

Medal of Distinction, General Conference Health Ministries Department (2004)

Medallion of Distinction, General Conference Education Department (2005)

Bridge Award, General Conference Communication Department (2005)

Plaques from General Conference Public Affairs and Religious Liberty Department

INDEX

PEOPLE
Adams-Wettstein, Suzanne 63
Aga, Negassa 55
Agnello, Silo 48
Aitken, James 108, 111
Anabaptists 122
Anastasio 48, 49
Archbishop of Canterbury 13, 56, 97, 98, 101, 115, 118, 136, 149, 152, 154, 159
Archbishop of Uganda 154
Bacchiocchi, Samuele 48, 57, 58
Baptists 20, 78, 80, 121-123, 153, 166
Barton, William 131
Basili, Metropolitan 126
Beach family 21-38, 44, 51, 62, 74, 91-100, 102, 131, 135, 136, 165-169, 171
Beaven, Winton 132
Beer, Luigi 49, 50
Benedict XVI 64, 101, 116
Bertalot, Robert 94
Blake, Eugene Carson 124
Bond, Linda 124
Brown, George 108
Bruinsma, Reinder 59
Buonfiglio, Michele 48
Cady brothers 40
Campbell, M. V. 163
Canterbury, archbishop of 13, 56, 97, 98, 101, 115, 118, 136, 149, 152, 154, 159
Carey, George 97, 115, 159
Catholics 50, 51, 73-79, 107, 113-117, 124, 136, 159
Ceauşescu, Nicolae 150
Cella, Flavio 48

Chalupka, R. 126
Chavez, Stephen (Steve) 7, 11
Christian, Percy 33, 54
Churchill, Winston and Randolph 20
Coggan, Donald 136
Congar, Ives 75
Conradi, L. R. 23
Copiz, Pietro 48
Copiz, Romeo 48
Corley, Artemus 93, 166
Corley, Bob 166
Corley, Bryan 165
Cossentine, E. E. 67, 68
Cotton, David Beach and Shery 169
Cullman, Oscar 74, 75
Cupertino, Giuseppe 47
Dabrowski, Rajmund (Ray) 103
Dabrowski, Stanislaw 80, 128
De la Hera, Alberto 159
De Meo, Giuseppe 48
Dewey, Thomas 135
Di Bartolo, Guiliano 84
Downing, Pilar Santandar 112
Dufau, André 44
Duke of Edinburgh 153
Duncan, I. Richard 37
Duprey, Pierre 159
Edinburgh, duke of 153
Elizabeth II 97, 152, 159
Enholc, Alexander 127
Eva, Duncan 69, 70
Fallon, Joseph 37
Fehrenbach, Marvin 35
Flachmeier, Ray 102
Fox, DeWitt 131
Friday, Lynn 82
Gafner, Eugen 37
Gallagher, Jonathan 112
Gandhi, Indira 154

Gandhi, Rajiv 154
Gao Ying 155
General Conference presidents 16, 53, 58, 82, 107, 124, 155
Gmünder, Samuel 25
Graz, John 14, 64, 86, 95, 122-124, 136, 162
Gregorios, Metropolitan Mar 74
Guddaye, Tebedge 87
Hale, Joe 131, 160
Halverson, Wilton L. and Hazel 37, 38, 54, 99
Hamer, Jerome 75, 76
Hamilton, L. Mark 35, 38
Hammill, Richard 78, 125
Harding, George T. 35, 37, 132
Harding, Warren G. 35
Hegstad, Roland 106
Herzog, Anny Tissot 164
Herzog, Hans (Hai) Beat 92, 164
Herzog, Hans Jőrg and Myrta 164
Hitler, Adolf 30-32
Hogganvik, Kristian 87
Houmann, C. J. 87
Ibrahim, Metropolitan Gregorios 98, 119
Ivy, Andrew 132
Jacobs, Lyndsay and Lorraine 160
Jaruzelski, Wojciech 126, 127
John XXIII 113
John Paul I 80
John Paul II 75, 101, 114, 115, 154
Johnsson, William 56, 95, 122, 124
Jones, E. Stanley 132
Jones, Harold T. 37
Jones, Pat 37
Jones, Ralph 37
Kampelman, Max 132
Karstrom, Henning 55

Kasper, Walter 115, 159
Kempf, Henri and Hilda 177
King, Martin Luther 154
Kisekka, Samson 142
Kloosterhuis, Robert 155
Kobia, Samuel 157
Koning, John 37
Kramer, Sid 130
Kűng, Hans 75
Kwasniewski, Aleksander 126
Lakey, Othal 102
Lanarès, Pierre 112
Landless, Peter 132
Lavanchy, Jean and Jaqueline 171
Lazar, Pavel 129
Lecoultre, Andre 94
Lee, Allen 160
Leiske, Albert 133
Leiske, Elizabeth (Betty) 133
Leiske, Robert (Bob) 133
Lenoir, Roger 51
Leopold III 52
Lindbeck, George 74
Lippolis Segni, Anna 59
Livingstone, David 24
Lohne, Alf 70, 71, 106
Lopatka, Adam 128
Lucchicchia, Elisena 58, 59
Luther, Martin 122, 150, 160, 164
Lutherans 74, 95, 122, 124, 127, 160
Lutz, Jerry 102, 134
Lyko, Zachariasz 126-129
Malik, Charles 79, 80
Mansfield, Gloria 82
Marchi, Graziano 48
Martinez de Codes, Rosa Maria 160
Matthews, James 131, 132
Mau, Carl 160
Maxwell, Arthur 78

McMillan, John 56
Meldrum, George 37, 38
Methodists 131, 132, 153, 160
Minnerath, Roland 98, 159
Moses, Michael 55
Murd, E. 79
Nichol, Francis D. 73
Nikodim, Metropolitan 79, 80
Noko, Ishmael and Gladys 160
Nowak, Karel 112
Nussbaum, Jean 42, 45, 46, 53, 94, 112, 113, 117, 154
Nyomi, Setri 162
Offseyer, Jordan 102
Olson, A. V. 29
Olson, Michael 102
Opocensky, Milan 162
Ostich, Mildred 39
Palange, Blanche 52, 53
Palange, Louis 51-53
Parsons, James C. 37
Paul VI 79, 113
Pedersen, Emmanuel W. 58, 100
Perret, Edmond 162
Peterson, John 102, 160
Pierson, Robert 124
Plumbley, Tom 102
Polok, Wladyslaw 126, 129
Popes 64, 75, 79, 80, 101, 113-116, 146, 152, 154, 164
Potter, Philip 161
Pradervand, Marcel 161
Presbyterians 25, 122
Presidents, General Conference 16, 53, 58, 82, 107, 124, 155
Presidents, U.S. 35, 115, 126, 135
Prime ministers 99, 142, 154
Prout, Chester 54
Radano, John 59
Rasi, Humberto 155

Renan, Joseph Ernest 23
Renouvin, Pierre 42-44
Riddles, Libby 174
Robeck, Mel 102, 160
Robert, Jacques 63
Robert, Marie-Caroline 63
Robinson, Don 156
Robinson, Elaine 59
Roosevelt, Eleanor 45, 94, 110
Roosevelt, Theodore 112
Ross, Gary 111
Rossi, Gianfranco 48, 50, 75, 84, 94, 98, 110, 112, 117, 154
Runcie, Robert 101, 152, 159
Samuel (bishop, Coptic Church) 154
Sawa, Metropolitan 126
Sbacchi, Alberto 48
Scharffenberg, W. A. 78, 132
Schlink, Edmund 74
Schroth, Reinhard 150
Schubert, Otto 46
Schweitzer, Albert 23, 24
Scragg, Walter 69, 106, 107
"Separated brethren" 77
Seventh Day Baptists 123
Shaffer, Blanche 159
Skarzinski 125
Sladek, O. 85, 86
Smith, Uriah 174
Stalsett, Gunnar 160
Stampp, Kenneth 42
Steed, Ernest 131, 132, 154
Stein, Esther 25
Stransky, Thomas 76
Sudduth family 40
Sustek, Miloslav 85, 86
Swan, Patricia (Pat) 59
Tanner, Mary 159
Tarr, A. Floyd 33, 57, 58, 67
Tarr, John D. F. 33, 35, 37, 95

Thompson, G. Ralph 101, 112
Thompson, Robert 40
Ting, K. H. 155, 156
Tolbert, William 153, 154
Trovall, Carl 102
Truman, Harry S. 135
Tucci, Roberto 79
Tveit, Olav Fykse 157
Udovich, Willy 48
Uganda, archbishop of 154
Unnersten, Roland 70, 71
Utt, Miriam 83
Vacca family 171
Verfaillie, Maurice 112
Verghese, Paul (later Metropolitan Mar Gregorios) 74
Victoria 23
Vincentelli, Mario 48
Vischer, Lukas 74, 121, 160, 161
Visser't Hooft, Willem 74, 157
Votaw, Heber 35
Walesa, Lech 126
Wallace, Henry 135
Warren, Earl 38
Watson, Charles 132
Watts, Isaac 179
Weidner, John 31, 74
Weigel, Gustav 75
Wettstein, Walter 63
White, Ellen G. 16, 17, 60, 65, 139, 143, 146, 177, 178
Willebrands, Johannes 75
Williams, Harry 124
Wilson, Nancy 15
Wilson, Neal C. 101, 107, 124, 154, 155
Wilson, Ted N. C. 15, 16
Wisniewski, Jan 128
Witt, Walter 112
Wong, Robert 156

PLACES
Aba, Nigeria 152, 181
Addis Ababa, Ethiopia 55, 87, 89
Alaska 102, 174
Alps, Bernese 92
Alps, French 19-21
Angwin, California 33-39, 54, 62, 83, 95, 132, 135, 148, 164, 182
Arezzo, Italy 84
Athens 151
Atlantic City, New Jersey 171
Austria 22, 29
Belgian Congo (now Democratic Republic of the Congo) 20, 52
Belgium 22, 23, 28-30, 44, 51-53, 62, 91, 93, 147, 166, 167, 171
   Belgian seaside 22, 23, 91
   Brussels 22, 44, 51-53, 62, 91, 93, 147, 167
Berkeley, California 41, 42
Berlin 30-32, 150
Bern 22-30, 35-37, 41, 48, 55, 61, 63, 71, 85, 91, 92, 161, 164, 167, 173
Berrien Springs, Michigan 57, 78, 121, 182
Bracknell, England 56, 57, 94, 168
Brussels 22, 44, 51-53, 62, 91, 93, 147, 167
Bouaké, Côte d'Ivoire 167
California 33-46, 62, 68, 95, 99, 123, 148, 152, 166, 168
   Angwin 33-39, 54, 62, 83, 95, 132, 135, 148, 164, 182
   Berkeley 41, 42
   Glendora 123
   Loma Linda 35
   San Francisco 37, 39, 54
   Stanford 38-42
Collonges, France 31, 47, 49, 57, 85, 121, 168, 172
Colombia 48, 50
Copenhagen, 75
Costa Rica 99
Côte d'Ivoire 167
Croatia 136, 151
Czechoslovakia 22, 71, 74, 85, 86, 104, 126, 150, 162
   Prague 71, 74, 85, 86, 104, 126, 150, 162
      Bethlehem Chapel 150
      Czech Republic Senate Chamber 86
Debre Tabor, Ethiopia 87
Denmark 24, 75, 136
England 13, 22-24, 29, 32, 59, 63, 70-73, 87, 124, 127, 151-156, 159, 165-168, 171
   Bracknell 56, 57, 96, 168
   London 13, 29, 73, 87, 127, 151-156
      Wesley's Chapel 153
   St. Albans 41, 167
   Watford 167
Eritrea 87, 90
Ethiopia 48, 55, 57, 68, 87-90, 177
   Addis Ababa 55, 87, 90
   Debre Tabor 87
   Kuyera 57
Europe 19-31, 35-38, 43-45, 56-58, 62, 67-75, 82, 85-87, 103-107, 125, 133, 144, 148, 154, 163-171
Finland 24, 38, 55, 68, 78, 125, 136, 159
Florence 15, 42, 46-49, 53, 54, 58, 59, 84, 93, 148, 164, 167, 168, 171
France 20-23, 28-31, 36, 41-49,

53, 56, 57, 61, 63, 74, 85, 94, 120, 121, 135, 151, 166-173
Collonges 31, 47, 49, 57, 85, 121, 168, 172
Paris 20-23, 41-46, 53, 56, 61, 63, 74, 94, 120, 151, 167, 170-173
French Foreign Ministry archives at Quai d'Orsay 42
Geneva, Switzerland 73, 74, 79, 111, 112, 118, 121, 124, 131, 132, 154, 161
Germany 22, 23, 28-32, 36, 64, 117, 122, 136, 150, 164
Berlin 30-32, 150
Berlin Wall 150
Wittenberg 150
Gland, Switzerland 20, 62
Glendora, California 123
Haskell, Texas 166
Hungary 22, 71, 104, 126
Iceland 100
Imo State, Nigeria 56, 181
Istanbul 123
Italy 15, 26, 29-31, 38, 40, 42, 46-51, 57-62, 67, 73, 84, 93, 94, 135, 151, 164, 167, 168, 171
Arezzo 84
Florence 15, 42, 46-49, 53, 54, 58, 59, 84, 93, 148, 164, 167, 168, 171
Rome 31, 57, 73-77, 84, 113, 115, 117, 132, 146-151, 156
Mamertine Prison 151
See also Vatican
Katanga 52
Kraków, Poland 154

Kuyera, Ethiopia 57
Lake Geneva, Switzerland 19
Liberia 153
Loma Linda, California 35
London 13, 29, 73, 87, 127, 151-156
Mars Hill, Athens 151
Maryland 33, 59, 67, 68, 73, 171
Michigan 57, 78, 121, 182
Moscow 78-80, 125, 126, 152, 155
Mount Blanc 19
Netherlands 22, 29, 53, 71, 136
Utrecht 53
New Jersey 171
Nicaragua 108, 109
Nigeria 56, 88, 152, 181
Aba 152, 181
Imo State 56, 181
Port Harcourt 88
North Dakota 19
Norway 24, 160
Odessa, Ukraine 80
Paris 20-23, 41-46, 53, 56, 61, 63, 74, 94, 120, 151, 167, 170-173
Poland 50, 71, 78, 85, 87, 103, 104, 125-129, 154, 181, 182
Kraków 154
Warsaw 78, 85, 103
Port Harcourt, Nigeria 88
Portugal 30
Prague 71, 74, 85, 86, 104, 126, 150, 162
Rome 31, 57, 73-77, 84, 113, 115, 117, 132, 146-151, 156
Russia 78-80, 125, 126, 152
Moscow 78-80, 125, 126, 152
Kremlin 155
St. Petersburg 78, 125
San Francisco 37, 39, 54

Santiago de Compostela, Spain 151
Scotland 38
Seville, Spain 53
South Africa 112
Spain 20, 30, 50, 53, 77, 78, 98, 151, 159, 160
  Santiago de Compostela 151
  Seville 53
St. Petersburg 78, 125
Stanford, California 38-42
Sweden 22, 24, 71, 76, 79, 80, 89
  Uppsala 71, 79, 80
Switzerland 19-31, 33, 35-37, 41, 47, 48, 51, 55, 61, 63, 71-74, 79, 91, 92, 111, 112, 118, 121, 124, 131, 132, 147, 148, 154, 161, 164-167, 173
  Bern 22-30, 35-37, 41, 48, 55, 61, 63, 71, 85, 91, 92, 161, 164, 167, 173
  Geneva 73, 74, 79, 111, 112, 118, 121, 124, 131, 132, 154, 161
  Gland 20, 62
  Lake Geneva 19
  Muri 53
  Zurich 54
Syria 118, 119
Takoma Park, Maryland 33, 59, 67, 68, 73, 171
Texas 20, 29, 93, 166
  Haskell 166
Ukraine 80
Uppsala, Sweden 71, 79, 80
Utrecht, Netherlands 53
Vatican 73-77, 101, 113-116, 159
  Sala Clementina 115
  Santa Marta 115, 116
  Sistine Chapel 113

Venezuela 48
Warsaw 78, 85, 103
Washington, D.C. 30, 33, 44, 76, 103, 108, 109, 124, 130, 131, 151, 157, 162, 169
Watford, England 167
West Africa 68, 69, 71
Wittenberg 150
Zurich 54

SCHOOLS
Andrews University 57, 78, 121, 182
Collonges Adventist Seminary 47, 49, 57, 85, 121
Columbia Union College 35, 59, 67, 171
Freies Gymnasium 25, 92, 164
Gregorian University 57
Gridley School, California 39, 40
Italian Union Training School (Villa Aurora) 15, 42, 46-49, 54, 84, 148, 168
Loma Linda University 35
Newbold College 56, 57, 94, 168
Pacific Union College 33-39, 54, 62, 83, 95, 132, 135, 148, 164, 182
  Foreign Mission Band 36
  4:00 a.m. Club 37
Paris, first-grade school in 23
Saleve Adventist University 168
Sorbonne, *see* University of Paris
Stanford University 38-42
Toivonlinna Junior College, Finland 68
University of Bern 161
University of Brussels 51
University of California at Berkeley 41, 42
University of Paris 20, 23, 42-45,

56, 63, 170-173
Salle Blumenthal 172
West Liberty Union School, California 39, 168

SDA CHURCH
Afro-Mideast Division 58
Belgian Conference 22, 53, 59
British Union Conference 56, 81, 148
Central European Division 22
Chico Seventh-day Adventist Church 40
Clinique La Lignière 19
Euro-Africa Division 23, 48
Franco-Belgian Union 23, 171
General Conference 13, 15, 20, 27, 35, 51, 53, 55, 58, 59, 64, 67, 70-78, 81, 82, 88, 100, 103-108, 111-114, 117-121, 124, 125, 130, 132, 136, 137, 144, 147, 148, 155, 161-163, 171, 182
    Communication Department 103, 107, 182
    Education Department 55, 67, 68, 89, 125, 155, 182
    General Conference Rules of Order 107, 137
    Health Ministries Department 51, 182
    Public Affairs and Religious Liberty Department 13, 15, 35, 64, 106-108, 111, 120, 162, 182
    Temperance Department 78
Inter-American Division 108
Italian Union 46, 47
Netherlands Union 59
North France Conference 23
Northern California Conference Education Department 39
Northern Europe-West Africa Division 69, 71, 72, 106, 107
Northern European Division 22, 35, 56-58, 67-69, 85, 86
    Education Department 68, 69
Polish Publishing House 128
Polish Union Conference 80, 125-127
Review and Herald Publishing Association 73
Skodsborg Sanitarium 75
Southern European Division 22, 29, 33, 42, 45, 62, 85

EVENTS
Aleppo consultation (Syria) 118, 119
Annual Council, General Conference 70
Biafran war 88
Buckingham Palace garden party 95, 152, 153
Calendar reform 117-119
Chambesy Consultation 118
Christian Peace Conference (Prague) 74, 104, 162
Colosseum commemoration of martyrs of twentieth century 115
Conference of Secretaries of Christian World Communions 5, 13, 63, 113, 181
Council of Constance 150
Dialogues 13, 14, 56, 121-124
Doctoral dissertation defense 172
Easter date fixing 117-119

Ecumenical Patriarchate of
    Constantinople 80, 123
Five-Day Plan to Stop Smoking
    51
Food rationing during World
    War II 28
General Conference sessions 33,
    43, 53, 62, 67, 68, 77,
    123, 136, 137, 160
Iditarod race 174
Lambeth conferences 136, 152
Mennonite World Conference
    122
Millennium celebration 115
Papal audiences 113-116
Religious liberty declaration of
    the United Nations
    General Assembly 110,
    111
Second Vatican Council 63, 73-
    77, 113, 117-120, 135,
    136
Solidarity movement (Poland)
    126
Three-Self Patriotic Movement
    (China) 155, 156
Uppsala assembly 76, 79, 80

PUBLICATIONS
Adventist Review 7, 56, 73, 121,
    135, 158
Bright Candle of Courage 136
Ecumenism: Boon or Bane? 136,
    158
French Historical Review 42
Life and Health 131
Life and Health (French) 31, 61
New Testament in Swiss-Bernese
    dialect 177
101 Questions Adventists Ask 136
Pattern for Progress 136

Rotating the World With Rotary
    136
Steps to Christ 177
Vatican II: Bridging the Abyss
    136

MISCELLANEOUS
Baptist World Alliance 153
Bibliotheque Nationale 43, 151
British Broadcasting Corporation
    (BBC) 30
British Museum 151
Christian World Communions
    113
Church of God (Seventh Day)
    123
Church of God, Worldwide 123
Computer literacy 82
Congress of Vienna 30
Cosmos Club 79, 109, 130-132,
    157
Council of Free Churches 71
Council on Interchurch/Inter-
    faith Relations 121
Economic and Social Council of
    the United Nations 111
Ecumenism 107, 136, 158
International Commission for
    the Prevention of
    Alcoholism and Drug
    Dependency (ICPA) 63,
    131, 132
International Religious Liberty
    Association (IRLA) 63,
    86, 98, 112, 119, 153-156,
    160, 182
Intesa (agreement with the state
    in Italy) 50
Library of Congress 41, 151
Muri Rotary Club, Switzerland 63
National Press Club 130, 131

Polish Bible Society 96, 127, 182
Rotary International 63, 107,
    130, 136, 151, 153, 176
  Rotary four-way test 176
Salvation Army 124
Swiss Broadcasting Corporation
    (SBC) 31
Swiss Council of Churches 161
United Nations 63, 94, 106, 108,
    110-112
World Alliance of Reformed
    Churches (WARC) 122,
    161
World Council of Churches
    (WCC) 56, 63, 73-76, 79,
    98, 118, 121, 122, 124,
    131, 157, 161
Worldwide Church of God 123